DEMOCRACY

DEMOCRACY

ITS DEFECTS AND ADVANTAGES

C. DELISLE BURNS

GYAN

Published by

GYAN

Gyan Publishing House
5, Ansari Road
Daryaganj, New Delhi-110002
Phone: 011-47034999, 9811692060
E-mail: books@gyanbooks.com

Distribution Network
gyanbooks.com
India, USA, Canada, UK, Australia

ISBN: 978-93-7447-355-9 (PB)

First Published, 1929

2nd Impression 2026

Printed at: Gyan Press, Delhi.

DEMOCRACY

Author: C. DELISLE BURNS

DEMOCRACY

ITS DEFECTS AND ADVANTAGES

BY

C. DELISLE BURNS

LONDON
GEORGE ALLEN & UNWIN LTD
MUSEUM STREET

PREFACE

Two points only are intended to be emphasized in this book—first, that a positive contribution of thought and action from every member of the Community is needed, if government, industry, and social culture are to develop, and secondly, that the common man has many abilities, hitherto unused, from which such contribution could be made. The fundamental issues of contemporary social life involve psychological factors, which can be rendered most easily in modern terms: and therefore the abilities of the common man are analysed in such terms as behaviour, complex, and mind-group. The common man is not, in fact, as isolated from his fellows in thought and act as used to be imagined, and in his social characteristics is his strength. Co-operation is more natural to him than to the exceptional man.

But clearly psychology provides only the basis, not the criterion of policy. Only a knowledge of factors such as the moral standard or beauty, which knowledge is sometimes called philosophy, can provide a criterion by which the many habits of men may be evaluated. To look to the common man for contributions of thought in public affairs implies a conception of the democratic ideal, not indeed as "mass rule", but as a general principle of social organization, according to which every man has a place in his own right, and none is only a tool for the advantage of others. But democracy has been misinterpreted, both by its advocates and by its opponents. Therefore it will be necessary to analyse the meaning of the ideal with regard, for example, to incompetent legislatures or bureaucratic castes. Societies influenced by the democratic ideal exist in Europe and America; but they include many characteristics due to earlier forms of social life, which may be the cause of their obvious defects. Opponents of democracy omit or misrepresent references to history. The incompetence of voters and representatives to-day is trivial by comparison with the incompetence of monarchs and their ministers in the past; and the distresses of to-day are light by comparison with the diseases and sudden deaths of the eras before the democratic ideal was accepted.

However, the present is not proved to be good because the past was worse. The defects of democracy must be acknowledged. It will be argued, therefore, that certain corrections of the current view of democracy as well as of the practices of democratic societies must be made. The principle of correction is democratic, since it is implied that more and not less of the abilities of the common man would be brought into play by any reform; and this principle is opposed to a traditional view of aristocracy or of heroes and exceptional men as the source of vigour and intelligence in social life. No one denies the great value of exceptional insight; but the place of exceptional men in society is in question, and it is hoped that that problem will form the subject of another study. The integration, in any case, of the exceptional with the common in a democracy is quite different from the instrumentalism of the common in an aristocratic system. It is certainly implied in the democratic tradition that the common man provides more than a following; but that again involves a psychological view of his abilities.

Experience of social life is the best source from which to draw ideals; and in this book the experience used is that of Western Europe. But the conclusions are intended to be applicable also to America and Asia. Clearly a wider or a different experience would correct some limitations in the argument: for corruption in public officials and other such factors in social life would indicate new problems of democracy. If, therefore, the examples used in what follows are chiefly British, the reader who belongs to another tradition may substitute for them examples from his own country without destroying the force of the argument in its application to all modern life. At all costs, vague, general statements about democracy should be avoided, which are uncorrected by continual reference to observation of the behaviour of those with whom one is in closest contact. The general principle, however, seems to hold good that democracy involves co-operation in daily acts.

As the argument rests upon the existence of abilities in the common man, it may appeal to the common man and thus be not a scholar's exercise but a motive force. It is not, however, rhetorical exhortation, but detailed reasoning, which should be regarded as implying a compliment to the reader, even if it increases the need for his attention. The book is the completion of a plan which was adopted in lectures on "Democracy: its defects and advantages", delivered by me in 1928–9 in Glasgow as Stevenson Lecturer in Citizenship.

C. DELISLE BURNS

LONDON, ENGLAND
May 1929

CONTENTS

DEMOCRACY

CHAPTER I

THE CRISIS

Is the common man able to understand and to contribute to policy in public affairs? Or must he be commanded for his good by superior persons?

The institutions of to-day are much more intricate than ever before. The issues, economic or political, are much more important; because a failure to deal with them may cause much more suffering than ever before. The banking system, for example, is less simple than it was in the days when Lombard bankers first did business in Lombard Street; the public health system is much more complicated than it was even fifty years ago; and the diplomacy of Governments may precipitate wars far more disastrous than the quarrels of mediæval kings. But the competition of financial groups, which may affect diplomacy, is not easy to understand: the credit system is difficult to control, and even public health organization needs special ability.

The common man, therefore, may be held to be naturally and inevitably quite incompetent for such diffcult tasks as government; and the actual distresses of to-day may be explained by reference to mistakes made by voters or to the defects in the tastes of those who buy shoddy goods and prefer childish amusements. The old faith in everybody, viewed from a distance and called "the people", is somewhat shaken. The abilities of the common man may not be such as to warrant a belief in the democratic ideal or to justify a policy formed under its influence.

It must be agreed, for the sake of a continuous argument, that the words used have a definite meaning; for the advocates as well as the opponents of democracy are often at cross purposes about words. Here, therefore, it will be assumed that by the common man is meant that part in each man, woman, or child which is blood and bone, which eats and sleeps and moves, occasionally works and plays, and is compelled, after some years of decreasing physical energy, to die. The proportion in each man which is thus "common" seems to differ in different cases and perhaps at different moments; but in every case the common part is large. Again, each man seems to have some special ability which distinguishes him from his fellows; but that ability is rooted in what is common. The nerve-tissues are set in the blood and bone. The whole man is not the common man, for in each there is some exceptional element of wisdom or folly; but no man is, in the main, either a genius or a fool. That is to say, every man is the common man; and the great majority who have in them little special ability are common men almost all over.

Further, a man who is a specialist in carpentry or in mathematics may be even less than a common man in politics or general culture; that is to say, the other part of him may be a fool. In most cases, however, the specialist in one sphere tends to be the common man in other spheres. And if one man writes a book and another reads it—both tests of endurance—the parts of each which are not writing or reading are similar to parts of dustmen and bankers, and not therefore to be despised.

It should be noted that the "average man" and the "man in the street" are not other descriptions of the common man, but are phrases describing an entirely different group of facts. The average man is a mathematical norm, which is no man at all: and the man in the street is only the man one passes and does not know. The more sacred and less abusive language of tradition is also to be avoided, for psychological reasons which will appear in the course of the argument; and therefore "the majority", the "mass", "the people", "public opinion", the "general will"—all these must be regarded for the present as ghosts. They should perhaps remain in tombs; but at any rate they should not be allowed outside the graveyards of commentary upon dead authorities.

The problems to be dealt with here are not controversies of scholars, but practical issues of contemporary social life. Not the meaning of words, but the nature of certain facts is to be discussed: and the central fact on which the argument rests is that part or element in actual men, that is in the writer or reader of this, which is called the common man. This is a psychological fact—a certain amount of bodily behaviour, some impulses or tendencies inherited and shared with many, some intelligence and some emotional reactions. The common man is socially adjusted by institutions or customs; and he is taken here with all his habits in him. There is an actual difficulty in organizing government, in producing or selling goods, and in spreading education. The question is whether the common man has any part to play in the solution of such difficulties—whether, indeed, the Nobodies count at all.

Again, the meaning of the phrase "the democratic ideal" must be decided, not by definition but by analysis of actual tendencies. We are all of us old enough to know the worst, but some of us still hope for the best. We have been brought to this particular time and place partly by a long train of natural causes, partly by the acts, desires, and fears of our ancestors and of ourselves in the past few years. It would be futile to cast the account now in order to discover whether the burdens we bear are too great to be outweighed by the benefits we receive. There are boots and bread available; and there is a sort of order and liberty. But none of us is the king or queen of fairy-tale, which we may have wished to be when we were very young; and many of us are so little what we should like to be that our only wisdom is to make the best of a bad job. Clearly we must move. Either we drift on the current of natural forces or we control, at least in part, our own future; but it may be assumed that most men in Western Civilization are trying somehow to make their own lives better in wealth or welfare.

Not how we came here or what we have, but where we are going to and what we may reasonably expect to get—that is the most interesting part of history; for time has not stopped, and the history of the next ten years is more exciting, if less obvious, than the history of the past ten years. It would be worth while to discover, as far as we can, both what better situation is attainable and what are likely to be the best means of attaining it. But we cannot start from "scratch". We are already committed to a course; and our ideal as well as our method must therefore have reference to the tendencies already operative in our institutions.

If we survey the life of men to-day, it stands in contrast with ancient times, and even with the life of a century ago. There are obvious differences. Aeroplanes and wireless have carried farther the transformation of social life which was begun by railways and telegraphs. But the mechanisms now available are less significant for our present purpose than the uses made of them. Not all these have been good. No doubt the social life which has been affected by the new mechanisms may be in some respects less excellent than some social life has been before; for in spite of new power available, poverty is perhaps more oppressive than it was at some dates in the past, and war is more terrible. But whatever the balance of good or evil, clearly social life to-day is different in some important aspects from what it has been in the past.

Historical contrasts with Greek or Roman or Mediæval times are not important for our present purpose. Even the contrast with the last century before the industrial era, which has been many times described, may be omitted here. But there is a contrast within the experience of those now living, which is important for our own control of the future. From that point of view two general characteristics of our present social life are significant: one is the extent to which a large proportion of the population in certain countries share in the benefits and have a "say" in the control of the situation; the other is the discontent with the result and criticism of the institutions through which this has been achieved. In a very loose sense of the word "democracy", these two characteristics may be described as the extension of democracy and the opposition to it. The democratic ideal is, therefore, used here to mean the emotional conception which has been at work in the extension of the franchise and the betterment of the conditions of life for all and sundry. There is actual experience on which the arguments for or against such an ideal can be based.

In the first place, a greater proportion of the population in certain countries share in benefits and the control of policy. For example, the increase in the extent of the political franchise is remarkable.[1] It is not assumed for the moment either that a vote is of any value or that the results of an extended franchise are necessarily good. Those issues must be discussed later. All that is now asserted is that the desire for a vote has led to a very great number having votes: that is to say, a great number are citizens and fewer are merely subjects in modern states. The most startling change is in the direct political power of women; for women now have the political franchise in all European States of the Northern tradition, in the United States and the British Dominions. Again, political institutions of the representative kind have been introduced in all the new States founded since the war, in Germany and Austria and within certain limits, in Russia.

The political franchise is only one sign of an increase in the numbers of those who have some "say" in policy or have some effectual claim to its benefits. Even in industry or

[1] See my summary of recent changes in *1918–1928: A Short History of the World*, p. 397 sq.

economic life generally, and in spite of the survival of primitive methods of organization, there is a less complete domination of large groups of men by a select few. The increase of trade unionism and of consumers' co-operative societies in most Western countries, and even in Japan and China, is significant of the same tendency as is to be seen in politics. Large sections of industry are now organized definitely in reference to the desires of the manual workers in them; and large-scale production has made available for great numbers a certain supply of necessities and amenities.

Thirdly, within the last twenty or thirty years general culture has been acquired by a large proportion of the population in those countries in which political and economic democracy has increased. This is in part due to State systems of education. More schools and more time at school for manual workers—these divide us altogether, not only from the classical and mediæval, but even from the early industrial civilization. And general culture is not due only to schooling. Communication has become easier and available enjoyments more varied. The Press, the cinema, and wireless, have spread a form of general culture. They have spread it very thin perhaps, and the culture is in some aspects objectionable; but that involves another problem. Undeniably a much greater proportion of the population has *some* culture.

The ideals implied in the action thus taken are often obscure, and the theories on which policies have been based have in some cases been crude. But in general terms the characteristic features of social life, thus described, may be said to be due to the influence of the democratic ideal. Democracy in practice is the hypothesis that all men are equal, which is used in order to discover who are the best.[1] It implies the irrelevance for public policy of distinctions due to birth or wealth, the removal of which clears the ground for important distinctions of ability—not necessarily superior and inferior

[1] This description is given by D. G. Ritchie.

ability, but ability to do one thing rather than another. Equality in the democratic ideal therefore means not the identical value of each with the other, but, first, the assumption in public policy that no man or group has inherited privileges, and, secondly, the assertion that a man who is a good carpenter is an integral part of the community, no less than the man who is a good poet. But clearly in some advocacies of democracy equality has meant that any man is good at any public function, which is nonsense; and demagogues have often used "equality" as an excuse for their mean suspicion of exceptional ability. The democratic ideal can easily be shown to be absurd, if such meanings are accepted. Similarly, liberty has been taken to mean that every fool should do what he thinks best; and the opponents of democratic equality have sometimes advocated liberty as the right to avoid social responsibilities. But liberty in the democratic ideal means ability to grow to one's natural height, to develop one's abilities—which can occur only in a social soil. And in this sense, not in the individualist sense, liberty is an aspect of the democratic ideal. But far the most fundamental characteristic of the democratic ideal is fraternity. This means, not sentimentalism, but acting as if one's actions were part of a whole with the actions of other men, co-operating in a common enterprise. The ideal, in this sense, is not fully operative; but it has been at work in the transformation of social life which has recently taken place.

A democratic society would be one in which the common man, that is to say the greater part of most men and indeed the whole of most men in so far as they have no special competence in public policy, is used as a source of knowledge and a direct and original contributor to action in the affairs of the State, industry, and education. And such a society would also be one in which each man used his special competence, however limited, for the promotion of the good of all others in the community who are, in respect of that form of competence, common men. Such would be an ideal; but it is not proposed here to describe Utopia. No such society is likely to exist within the next ten years. Nor does the argument of this book lead to a philosophy of social life in general, although such a philosophy is implied. The immediate aim is to discover only what would be a situation better than the present in certain definite particulars. Such a situation would clearly not be permanent; but it is conceived as the next step. For that reason, the question arises whether the next step ought to be another step under the guidance of the democratic ideal already operative in certain communities. In spite of all the achievements which the nineteenth century would have called "progress", men are not more satisfied; for indeed one of the significant differences between yesterday and to-day is restlessness.

In the early stages of the process by which the present world was made, in the nineteenth century, the poets and scientists shared with the common man a benignant complacency. The mind of that time was childishly satisfied. Western Europe was said to be "the heir of all the ages, in the foremost files of time"; and Evolution, which quite unphilosophically was assumed to be identical with Progress, was felt to be justified, in spite of its red tooth and claws, when the side-whiskers of the mid-Victorians, the lace curtains and the aspidistras of that engaging civilization were seen to be its results. Alas! we are more doubtful now about our own excellence. A few Americans still preserve the complacency of that earlier time; but even Nordics seem to have had their confidence shaken. It is not only that we have not enough of what we desired in an extended franchise and cheaper goods; it is that some have begun to have doubts whether such things are desirable. Not merely the limited results of the ideal are criticized, but the ideal itself. We perceive that time has not stopped. Some with horror and some with relief have discovered that we are not the final results of human history, still less of the world-process. Those who are horrified, looking through whiskers and lace curtains, perceive that the youth are not doing what their fathers did, and are filled with despondency at modern decadence. The world, they say, is going to the dogs—assuming unworthy habits among dogs.

On the other hand, some who watch the change are only too well aware that the nineteenth-century heaven had below it a hell called the industrial city area. And even the angels who lived behind the lace curtains stood armed; for if there was one belief more firmly accepted by the nineteenth century than the belief in making money, it was the belief that some-one else wanted to take it away. The nineteenth century was no worse than the eighteenth, or the fourteenth or the fourth. The point is that among its achievements were many failures —failures of perception rather than of desire or achievement; and some, who now discover that the world is going on and that others coming after us may fare better, are believed to feel that civilized life is still a primitive art. The defects of the nineteenth century are now apparent even to those who admire its achievements. Thus, precisely at the moment when we might, if the ideals of that earlier time were adequate, have rested from our labours, we are aware of still more fundamental issues.

The undeniable defects of the existing situation have led not simply to hopes of something better, but to direct con-demnation of the methods we have been recently using; and as examples of such condemnation we may select two types of criticism of what is, for purposes of abuse, called by its critics "democracy". In their criticism the mean streets and narrow minds of to-day are assumed to be due to democracy; and most of our present ills are put to the debit of the common man.

One type of criticism is scholarly, the other popular. The former is based upon a standard of culture, the latter upon effectual force. The former is expressed in the traditional attacks on democracy of which the most powerful in recent times has been that of Emile Faguet, in his *Cult of Incompetence*. This repeats the old charges against men who do not write books, who are said to vote foolishly, to work incompetently, and to enjoy only what is barbaric. But it is assumed by such critics that these defects, undeniably prevalent in autocracies, were not serious until the common man was given or took power over public policy; for now, it is said, the common man's defects corrupt all social life and destroy the excellences of the exceptional.

The argument is this. Most men are unskilled or incompetent in large issues of public policy; and if they are given power to choose the man who is to control public policy, they choose the incompetent, because he is nearest to them, most intelligible and most controllable. Thus we have a cult of incompetence. Even the competent may have to pretend to be incompetent in order to be chosen for controlling the situation, if choice by the mass of voters is the only method of obtaining such control. Thus the whole State is ruined because it is not guided by those few who have a special competence in public affairs.

Against this argument two objections can be urged. If choice of leaders or governors is in fact incompetent, education of voters or choosers can make it more competent. It is foolish to condemn a system which has never been tried; and the assumption on which rests the practice of choice is that choosers can become more intelligent. It may be, therefore, that we have had not too much but too little democracy, especially as the defects in the choice made may have been due to the amount of energy spent in confusing the issues presented to those who are to choose. Again, defects in choosing are notoriously greater in countries in which popular choice is new, in which therefore autocracy has been prevalent; and therefore the defects in choosing may be due to the results of autocracy, not of democracy. However, that reply is not final; for it may be that most men are not in fact capable of education in public affairs. The problem remains therefore—what are the abilities of the common man? Is he or is he not capable of more than he does at present?

But a second objection can be urged against the view that popular choice is incompetent. What is competence? The intellectualist scholar and the specialist in any given problem tend to forget that men are chosen as representatives or leaders in politics, not as intelligent but as intelligible. Now in politics and industry and education the competent person may be, not the man who knows theory, but the man who can sway other men; for the "instrument" in social life is the common man and the common man is moved by those who can make themselves intelligible, who are therefore, in this sense, competent. Clearly the man chosen by the people must be popular, but "popular" is a term of abuse only among those who despise the people. It is regrettable if a man who is intelligible, is not intelligent; but it is equally regrettable if one's wisdom cannot be made perceptible to anyone but one's self. The complaint made by superior persons against democracy is often due to the inability of the complainant in making himself understood; but surely it is unfair to an audience to assume that, if they do not understand you, it is *their* fault.

Again, it is said against democracy that the civilization it produces is banal, mediocre, or dull. This is supposed to be due to the levelling down of genius or exceptional ability by the pressure of majorities. It is supposed that the common man is afraid of what is unusual and resents what seems in any way superior. Hence come homogeneous clothes and houses, forming homogeneous minds. Social life is reduced to the few and simple contacts of undifferentiated units. A democratic equality destroys all quality in an indiscriminate quantity of copies of a bad pattern; and the operation of the democratic ideal in the nineteenth century has, therefore, caused bad art and vulgar manners. A reply can be made. First, the undoubted mediocrity of some aspects of modern life may be due not to social pressure, but to natural causes or unintended, incidental results of actions which aimed at quite different ends. For example, homogeneous houses were clearly due to the pace at which the population grew in the nineteenth century. True, the architectural imagination might or should have kept pace with the need; but the fact that it did not cannot be put down to democratic pressure. Again, ugly clothes may be due to inefficient production, not degraded taste. Nobodies have little enough choice of alternatives in clothing; why therefore blame them for their choice? The defects in present taste, then, may be due to the failure of superior persons to dominate the new conditions.

Further, the reply to all doubts in regard to the treatment of the exceptional is to be found in the reasonable demand that the exceptional shall accept some social responsibilities. Common men quite rightly level down a superiority which repudiates the labour upon which exceptional skill depends. And they are right; for the assumption that fine ladies justify or excuse a slave population is difficult to accept as civilized.

Such arguments against the democratic ideal and the replies to them are given here only in order that the issue to be discussed in what follows may be understood. It is not pretended that either the opposition to or the advocacy of democracy have been so far fairly stated. But if the force of the arguments against democracy has been very obvious in a series of great books during the nineteenth century, it is no less obvious that the general tendency in most countries during that very century has been in favour of what the critics disliked. It would be impolite to suggest that the scholarly critics of democracy were intellectually survivals of an obsolete civilization, because they themselves learnt from the books of dead men and not from the talk of those despicable contemporaries of theirs who supplied their bread and boots. But even Plato and Aristotle had the defects of intellectualism; for they praised the city-state in a world in which it was already obsolete.

The real trouble, however, is not with scholars. The impatience at democracy seems to be due to an inability of the ambitious to get what they want. The charge of incompetence in choosing leaders or of levelling down ability comes from those who are not chosen or from those who feel that their ability is not recognized. But the consciousness of one's own worth, however correct, is an insecure basis for condemning those who are unable to see it. The practical issue is not whether the critics of democracy are correct in their assumption that they know what the best kind of ability is, but who is to call the tune.

The most serious attack on democracy, however, is made by those who find the reasons for their attack after it has succeeded. This second type of criticism is expressed in Fascism and Communism. Both these revivals of old creeds assert or imply that the common man does not in fact know what is good for him, and that institutions or habits, resting on the assumption that he does know, are either fraudulent covers for an actual autocracy or inevitably destructive of the common man's happiness. As an alternative, it is proposed that "the conscious minority", who know what is needed and how to get it, must take control of public policy and, therefore, of such peace or prosperity as is good for the common man. It must be assumed for the sake of the argument that this policy is not itself fraudulent—a cover for the desires of a person or a group to capture the "swag". Let it be granted, therefore, that the alternative to democracy may be a dictatorship which is benevolent.

For the moment the simple faith of Fascist or Communist is not questioned. Neither doubts that the actual few to which he belongs is the particular minority which knows what is best for all. Such faith is doubly strong if the Fascist or Communist group is actually in control; for the fact that it is in control is taken as proof that it ought to be in control, exactly as Aristotle proved that some men are naturally slaves by assuming that those who were slaves ought to be slaves. But it is possible to admit that only a few know what is needed and yet to doubt whether the Fascists or the Communists are those few, just as it is possible to agree with Aristotle that some men are naturally slavish and yet to discover these men among the masters. The faith of the "conscious minority" in their own competence is not easily acquired by the others, if the grounds for regarding the minority as competent are not even discussed by these others. It is possible to doubt the competence of those who will not allow their competence to be questioned; for even if criticism must be suppressed because incompetent persons may be misled by bad arguments, nevertheless to suppress criticism implies that those who suppress it are not competent enough to counteract what is misleading. The few actually in control in any community may not be those who ought to be in control, if the criterion is the best form of civilized life available, unless it is assumed that what is, is best. And even the Fascist or the Communist should admit this in their own case, since they assume it when they attack democratic societies actually in existence. The conscious minority in control, therefore, may not know what is good for the whole nation.

But on the main point, that the common man does not know what is good for him or how to get it—this depends on one's judgment of what the common man actually got when he was free to get it. And if he was never free, his competence has not been tested. But the best way of testing competence is to leave men free to make mistakes. Democracy, therefore, however despicable as a system of government, is better than dictatorship as a test of competence among common men; and it is fantastic to suppose that it has been tried in Italy, Russia, or Spain. That common men have proved to be gullible and indolent with regard to public affairs may be due to the fact that the wrong tests have been applied. Even the acknowledged failures of partial democracy, therefore, do not show that the only alternative is rule by a "conscious minority", dictators in the name of the Proletariat or of God or of the Nation.

Another argument against the democratic ideal is that it does not allow for the "sense of the community" or for the unity of the national spirit, since it splits society into segregate individuals, each seeking his own gain. A dictatorship, on the other hand, is said to hold men together by a common loyalty. This argument contradicts the cultured opponents of democracy above referred to, because they complain that liberty is destroyed by democracy, while dictators complain that liberty is too great under democracy. Obviously whatever the superior person dislikes, he calls democracy. But on the main issue, individualism is not democracy because it underrates the dependence of one man on another for the development of the abilities of each. The sense of the community, however, may be deficient in any society or nation because its members are unable to understand any unity but that of a flock of sheep. The unity of a nation may be one of many different kinds of unity. The unity of a mob of followers is natural to a dictatorship; but there is a form of unity in which equals co-operate in a common task, and that is democratic. It is not true, then, that no form of unity or of the sense of the community can exist except under a dictatorship: and, indeed, the force of the argument in what follows rests upon the competence of the common man for achieving higher forms of social unity.

It must, however, be admitted that in some communities common men are not competent to co-operate in government by the traditional methods of democracy. That is the basis of the new methods of colonial government, to which reference is made below. And it is possible that, even among European or quasi-European communities, the general level of culture is so low that "colonial" government for them is best. But that would imply a more primitive stage of government than democracy, and would hardly be welcomed as a justification for the utility of dictatorship, whose apologists pretend to have passed beyond democratic methods. What is here called "colonial" government in fact has no justification at all except as a step towards democratic government among communities whose form of social organization does not "fit" very well with the other forms prevailing in the world. The only valid argument therefore in favour of Fascism or Communism would imply that the countries to which they are applicable are not yet civilized.

Actual experience, however, provides a test of the kind of competence which dictatorships are supposed by their advocates to possess. It is worth noting that the killing or maiming or the imprisonment of those who cannot be persuaded, indicates a lack of competence in the art of persuasion. A boxer may be more competent, by such a test, than a poet; and if boxing rather than poetry is conceived to be useful in government—that indicates a primitive conception of government. Government is the "moving" of men; and a man may be "moved" either by a blow or by an emotional appeal. But if a man is pushed and pulled, he is treated as not a man, that is to say, unskilfully; and if he is "influenced", his own inner force is used—which is both more economical in energy and more productive of the common force in society. Now democracy is nothing but the use of the inner motive force in each man, which inner force is untouched by the external pressure of the authority of superior persons, who are incompetent to persuade and must therefore compel.

The competence, on the other hand, claimed for dictatorship is largely mechanical. It is the sort of competence which prison-warders may possess. Hours and work are regular and food is adequate; and the absence of independent thought may be good for the prisoners—as prisoners. Or again, competence to make a railway keep time or a post office deliver letters is quite admirable, but somewhat limited in range. That such competence should be highly praised indicates the low standard of those who praise it, if that is all they expect from government and industry; but it cannot prove dictatorship more competent than democracy in the finer skill by which men are influenced.

The underlying assumption in the arguments of Fascism and Communism, however, is that the common man not only does not know, but *cannot discover* what is good for him. The democratic ideal is not proved to be futile because it has not been achieved; for at that rate one should not attempt to build a ship because it is not already built. But Fascists and Communists do not appear to act always on the assumption that there is nothing more in the common man than has already been used. Both Fascists and Communists in practice devote much time to what they call education; and it is admitted that education tends to bring into play some abilities not otherwise available. Therefore both Fascism and Communism imply that there are abilities of common men which have not so far been used. On the other hand, the educational system under a dictatorship differs fundamentally from that which operates under the influence of the democratic ideal, because in a dictatorship the particular abilities which are needed are assumed to be known. In Communism the education is "Marxian", in Fascism it is nationalist. Clearly in both cases the truth is assumed to be known. But in a democracy this is not assumed; and the opponents of democracy quite misunderstand it, if they imply that there is a democratic doctrine similar to the Marxian or the Fascist. The democratic faith is that correct doctrine will be discovered if all possibilities of error are explored; but the belief implied in dictatorship is that exploration is unnecessary because all is discovered. Those who know much know how little is known. The ignorant are dogmatic. Indeed, as the advocates of Fascism say, it is precisely the young and the untrained mind which is attracted by an established doctrine.[1] The maintenance, therefore, of quasi-educational methods for producing either Marxians or Fascists is no proof of a belief in the education of unknown abilities: it is only a trick for the formation of passive instruments for a fixed policy.

But in the experience of all such methods, the attempt to form a fixed belief in established doctrine and a particular type of human instrument has always failed. The reason is psychological. To present a doctrine requires commentary; and the more commentary, the more easily the mind escapes from the text. Therefore any education at all is dangerous to any system but a democracy, as indeed is recognized by those who hesitate to educate "lower orders". Again, as to types of character and conduct formed by education—much can be done to twist muscles or deaden perception; but the more rigidly the psychological forces in a man are canalized, the less capable the man becomes to stand new strains or face unprecedented issues. Communities stiffened by a single faith are less powerful in changing circumstances than communities within which many different faiths and many different types of character exist. But there is no possibility that the future will be identical with the present, and the common man also inevitably changes. The assumption, therefore, that the common man cannot know what he does not now know and cannot do what he has not so far done, implies either that the competence to teach is inadequate—as appears to be the case in dictatorships—or that every possible method has been already tried, which is childish.

Finally, any dictatorship which assumes the essential incompetence of most men may imply that it exists without any popular support, which dictators are unwilling to assert because they desire popularity as a form of power. But if the dictatorship has popular support, then it is supported,

[1] Rocco *Pol. Doctrine of Fascism.* Internat. Council. Doc. No. 223. Oct. 1926.

on its own showing, by those who are incompetent to know what is good for them. Thus a dictatorship popularly supported would be better if the support were competent; but that, on the assumption of dictatorship, cannot be brought about. The only reasonable course, therefore, for dictatorship implies the correctness of the democratic ideal and the confession of inability to apply it. The fundamental issue remains—Are there abilities in the common man, still unused, which may provide competence in public affairs?

The doctrines of the advocates of dictatorship, however, are not important. All have been refuted many times already. Nor are the minor successes of dictatorship in certain countries, where political training has been notoriously defective, such as to indicate any danger to the democratic ideal or even to the partial expression of that ideal in traditional parliamentarianism. But the practical methods of certain able dictators suggest the problems which the common man has to face in the next ten or twenty years; and the exposition of the chief arguments for dictatorship as at present practised is intended to indicate the actual issues of to-day, which affect social life in its three chief phases, the political, the economic, and the cultural. The disappointment at the results so far attained under the influence of the democratic ideal and the open hostility to that ideal among undeveloped populations do not prove the ideal itself to be futile; but they indicate the need for further examination of its meaning and more skilful choice in the means for attaining it.

We are faced by problems of government, of industrial organization, and of education. Certain great evils have to be overcome in each sphere, which are obviously more ancient than any form of democracy, for example, war and poverty. But that is not the only issue. Modern government is a means for improving public health as well as preventing violence. Modern industry is a means for producing and using more and better goods and services by extended mechanization and more comprehensive organization; but it is also a means for higher development of human capacities in the arts of production and use. Modern education is a means for increasing the supply of available competence in the maintenance and development of civilized life. But to express the problems of government, industry, and education in terms of human abilities not yet fully developed, implies the acceptance of the democratic ideal as a guide in the devising of public policy in each of the three spheres of social life. The precise place of the common man in all these spheres can be discovered by observation of contemporary experience; and the abilities of the common man not yet available may show themselves under the operation of the democratic ideal in the devising of policy. The first step, then, is the analysis of the abilities available.

CHAPTER II

PSYCHOLOGICAL ABILITIES

If the defects of democracy do not show that we are on the wrong road, still less that we must return to forms of aristocratic culture and oligarchic rule, what is to be done? Can we do better in civilized life than the immediate past has done? It is not a question for our children's children. Whatever one thinks of the new generation, we are not dead yet; and the issues involved in persistent evils must be faced within the next ten years. Of these evils the greatest at the moment are poverty and war. But if they should be abolished, it is not only because distress may cause revolution or a future war stop dog-racing. Whether the future effects of poverty and war are important or trivial, one of the chief reasons for abolishing them is the existing waste of human ability which the continuance of these two primitive institutions involves. The reasons for action, therefore, are not to be sought only in ten years' time or in hidden slums. These reasons are obvious here and now, here in comparative comfort and now when this is being read. The present situation is defective because of the poverty daily destroying abilities which arise among those for whom conditions of life provide too little sustenance. The waste of human material diminishes the resources available for the whole community. And war, from which we now suffer, is not the mere dropping of bombs, but the waste of energy, intelligence, and material, in absurd preparations for killing other men who are preparing to do the same to us. It is not only the waging of war, but also the preparation for war which should be abolished. Such evils, however, can be abolished only by radical changes in social custom and in current intelligence and emotion. In order that these changes may occur in social life, there must be a clearly conceived attainable state of society, for the foundation of which public policy and private action can be effectual. Conditions other than those over which men have control must obviously be favourable. But these are assumed for the present purpose to be at least sufficiently favourable for such policies as are to be discussed. It is assumed, for example, that the world will not end to-morrow and that no great natural calamity will sweep away the necessary intelligence and ability. That is to say, cataclysms are discounted. Modifications in our plans will have to be made, if the next ten years are altogether unlike the past in such matters as the dryness of the seasons or the resistance of the human body to attacks by bacteria. But such possibilities are noted only in order that the larger world in which human history occurs may not be forgotten. The human part of history is in our control.

Within the area under our control the most important factors are ideals—that is to say, emotional conceptions of a better state which are capable of moving men to act. And the particular group of such conceptions which have been operative in the recent past have been called above by the one name—democracy.[1] Psychologically the democratic ideal may not have been formulated until after the effect of certain tentative efforts had succeeded in turning public policy towards the interests of common folk and in increasing the activities of such folk in public affairs. But psychological forces in the common man have been operating to produce those characteristics of contemporary society which are called democratic; and these forces must be analysed and made emotionally

[1] See John Dewey, *The Public and its Problems*, p. 148. "Regarded as an idea, democracy is not an alternative to other principles of social life. It is the idea of community life itself. It is an ideal in the only intelligible sense of an ideal: namely, the tendency or movement of something which exists carried to its final limit, viewed as completed, perfected. . . . Wherever there is conjoint activity whose consequences are appreciated as good by all singular persons who take part in it, and where the realization of the good is such as to effect an energetic desire and effort to sustain it in being just because it is a good shared by all, there is in so far a community. The clear consciousness of a communal life in all its implications constitutes the idea of democracy."

more effectual. It is assumed, no doubt, even in proposing such a task that knowledge of manners and customs, institutions and beliefs, can be carried further and—more important still—that there is a store of energy which has not yet been made available, which may be used for improving the situation. But such assumptions are generally granted. Most men will allow that more may be known and that we are not altogether exhausted or decadent as a race. In any one country or nation, indeed, there may be no further supply of intelligence and an insufficiency of idealistic impulses; although probably even in countries charged with such defects, only a small and decadent group is actually defective. But the only way of proving whether or not we can know more or do more is to try; and it is, after all, not too much to give ourselves the credit of being supposed to be alive until we can no longer protest against being treated as dead. British industry, for example, has often been laid out for its funeral, but it has hitherto sat up again. Those who propose to regard us as dead are open to the suspicion that they would prefer us so. But we may surely be pardoned for taking another view. It is not unreasonable, therefore, if the democratic ideal is not yet fully operative, that we should use whatever life is in us to reform our social life under its inspiration.

Omitting for the moment the task of making the ideal clearer, it should be understood that what is to be discussed here is what is attainable. Utopia is not the present subject. It is not suggested that work should be done for a society which could not conceivably be better. The state of society attainable within our lifetime is not likely to be a heaven on earth. It is proposed, however, to consider how there may be a situation better than the present in certain definite features. Such a situation—for example, without poverty and war—would be better because it would involve greater benefits more generally shared and less "cost" or less unevenly distributed burdens in its maintenance or development. How much greater the benefits would be and how much less the cost, can hardly be calculated now. The little improvement that is attainable soon may seem to many not worth troubling about, if indeed only a little can be done. But it cannot be proved, and it must not be assumed that only a little difference can be made. The amount of difference attainable clearly must depend, if not on our knowledge of conditions, at least upon the energy available for bringing it about; and it is precisely that which is underestimated by those who despise the common man.

But the positive characteristics of that new and better situation must not be interpreted only in terms of greater benefit and less cost; because such terms may be misunderstood. True, the attainable ideal may be more food or less labour, more cinemas and less monotony—but these "goods" are meaningless except in reference to the appetite for enjoyment or the zest of living which they satisfy. Therefore, the better situation must be described in terms of living men and women and children. The actual persons living ten years hence must be conceived, not only as having more, but as being capable of using more; that is to say, as more alive. Not merely a larger amount of energy or vitality, but a finer quality of personality, character, or perceptiveness, is the characteristic of that better situation which is here taken to be attainable.

The resources available for contending with evils and increasing vitality are not merely so much economic wealth or political experience, but also the enthusiasms or ideals of common men, whatever these may be. Reforms obviously cost money, and better administration depends upon the flexibility of political institutions; but if there is not enough passion and intelligence, no mechanism or institution will be effectual. Again, however, it is clear that we cannot tell how much ability is available until we attempt to use it.

It follows that both in estimating our resources for improving the situation and in inquiring into the character of the new situation at which we aim, psychology is needed. Not learned jargon, but exact observation of men and women and children in their natural human relations—that must be the basis of the art of living in society; and, no doubt, many practical politicians, employers, and trade unionists, know psychology in this sense, although they have never heard their knowledge of men called by that name. The name is dangerous. Indeed the traditional psychology was not only defective but actually misleading as a basis for policy. It misrepresented men. It attended too much to sense-perception, which is perhaps the most individualized of mental processes, and neglected instincts and impulses in which a man lives with his race or his group. It implied that reasoning was calculation and ignored sympathy and imagination; and it established a fantastic mythology of conscious "will", made still more fantastic when applied to large groups of men as "the will of the people" or "public opinion". For the understanding of the facts of social life and for controlling them in a policy, it is necessary to avoid such phrases because they imply a misleading psychology. But the psychological knowledge of practical men is not abolished by the new development of the science. It is explained and carried further by modern experimental methods and by the analysis of behaviour.

This reference to a new theory should not, in releasing us from one jargon, imprison us in another. The jargon of psychoanalysis and of behaviourism may be no less dangerous than the abstractions of the traditional psychology. If men are not merely nerves for sense-perception nor calculating machines, neither are they sex-maddened anthropoid apes, who cannot help themselves when the weather changes. Indeed, modern psychology should have shaken the self-confidence of psychologists; but instead—those who study the strange sources of other men's beliefs seem to be all the more dogmatic about the excellence of their own. There is more real psychological observation in contemporary drama, novels, and poetry than in all the psychological treatises; and the psychological "treatment" in the common man's conversation is more skilful than the probing of the psychotherapeutic doctor. Some general statement, however, can be made in modern terms, which may indicate the kind of abilities in the common man which are available. This is not a contribution to psychological science, nor even an addition to social theory, but merely a statement in summary form of what is generally recognized. It is proposed, then, to review the abilities of the common man in order to discover what forces maintain the present structure of society and what are available or may be made available for improving it. That it can be improved has been already indicated in what has been said above as to the existence of ideals and of their influence.

A man thinks and feels in his blood and bone. He does not think or feel less, but more deeply, if he digs coal or drives a train. Mental activity is not only in the nerve-endings, but throughout the whole body; and, indeed, those who are sometimes called "intellectuals", who think and feel mainly with the "grey matter" and not with the body-muscles, are generally superficial in their sympathies and unstable in their opinions. Most psychological science and all political and economic theories have been the work of intellectuals, who not unnaturally often ignore the blood and the bone. They have tended, therefore, to underestimate the extent of what is common and to put too much emphasis upon the exceptional. The behaviour of the common man, which in a sense is his mental life, is best to be seen in his walking and speaking and habitual occupation, and not so clearly in crises such as elections or strikes. The movement of blood and bone, in which nerves are set, is social. A man is not a unit who acquires social habits. He does not discover his race; he is a discovery of his parentage and his group. The intellectual's independence is abnormal. The abilities of men normally arise in a society of men. Mental activity is essentially social. Minds are fundamentally in contact, one with another. Thinking and feeling are always social; for language, of which the chief purpose is communication, delimits all actual thinking and the stimulus to feeling is a selection probably made by one's parents or earliest companions.

Beneath or behind all conscious perception are the unconscious tendencies and impulses, some few of which are "in play" in any form of social life, which is called a civilization; and these tendencies and impulses are shared. No man would have them in this or that form unless other men with whom he is in contact so had them. Even seeing a red patch, a process with which the older psychologists played, is less simple, less fundamental, less human, than the shared impulses of that blood and bone which is "spirit". The roots out of which come political passion and economic activities and the finest flowers of art are deep down in all men, underlying all their differences, and certainly deeper than sense-perceptions and the reasonings built upon them. Social custom and daily habit, upon which institutions rest, are imbedded like roots in blood and bone, which are physically similar in most of the members of any stable population. But that does not imply inevitable traditionalism; for the atmosphere and soil, which are the blood and bone of the common man, contain very much more than is expressed or embodied in any actual institutions.

Secondly, the life of men in society is not all at one level. There are ups and downs. A man or a group of men may at one moment be deeply moved and at another hardly alive. A group may be at one moment in loose contact and at another, for example, in some common danger or under stress of some appeal, closely knit. Individuality and sociability are not stable or continuous; they are transient factors in the whole of social life. It is therefore equally true to say that democracy is mob-rule, or that the voice of the people is the voice of God; but each is true only of a particular situation, and neither is always true.

The study of abnormal states of mind has increased our respect for extremes. Normal life is seen to be not a mere succession of similar movements, but as fluctuating as a flame in a wind. We never see all that is to be seen nor feel all that can be felt, and in most men at most times and in most situations the range of percipience is comparatively small. Not only are the normal senses restricted, so that only some of many colours or sounds are perceived; but in most of life we do not grasp what other men are thinking or feeling. Occasional flashes outside or occasional increases of inner vitality move, like waves on a sea, across the current of daily experience. That is the life of common men. There are times in which men who are not exceptionally able can see very keenly and feel very deeply; and a dictator who desires to use them merely as his instruments may find the tool turning in his hand. The democratic ideal, on the other hand, implies that the instrument is alive all through; and this is psychologically valid.

Thirdly, there is a mental structure or "set" formed by what are called "complexes", groupings of emotional susceptibilities or sentiments, of ideas and of habitual behaviour-patterns or ways of acting. Mental life is no longer conceived as a bag full of ideas and sensations. Mental structure is formed long before there is any consciousness of a separate self; and most mental structure is social, in the sense that what is called one man's mind is part of a structure, of which the other parts are what are called other men's minds. Families and groups of factory workers and nations are mental structures, amenable to some influences and not to others. One such structure may be adaptable to Fascism, another to Communism; and other social mental structures may not be adaptable to either. The tendencies that make for war are set in mental structures lying much deeper down in the common man than the reasons given for preparing for war. Experience of past dangers survives a change of circumstances. The common man is not *materia prima*, or formless protoplasm for manipulation by leaders and great men. We cannot in any country or race begin from creation out of nothing; and although any group is flexible if the correct method is used, no group is completely elastic. Indeed, in many cases the influence of a leader seems to be hardly more than the expression of a tendency which he perceives in the behaviour of common men. Thus, the conception of mental structure and complexes which are social may be useful for indicating the limits of what is probable in any group or community.

But by far the most important contribution to the social sciences made in abnormal psychology is the suggestion that the abilities now "in play" are not all that may be made available. The current forms of social life canalize some of our abilities to see, hear, or feel, to speak or to work; but this canalization does not bring in all the waters to run the machinery. Some tendencies or impulses are sublimated or changed in direction; others are perhaps given only small outlets—as it were, wasted in frivolous or unsatisfying habits; and others again may be repressed. It is not a condemnation of the past to say that what men hitherto found it necessary to repress may be now released to do new work. Clearly, there have been wasteful or ruinous repressions; for most men nowadays would agree that the burning of heretics was altogether wrong, not merely because we find that method ineffectual for maintaining truth but also because it is wasteful of possible contributions to the common store. Most men nowadays would agree that the puritanical fear of the theatre and the parental domination over children were repressions altogether unnecessary, if not actually pernicious. And in the mind of any one person a repression of speech about sexual facts may narrow the growth of mental life. In many ways, therefore, the abilities of men are limited by repressions of tendencies, some of which may have been harmful, others merely alarming to the ignorant or the timid.

But apart from inherited or generally accepted repressions, clearly it may be necessary to repress for new purposes some impulses and tendencies. Head-hunting and witch-burning and bayonetting, although they would be enjoyed by a few men even to-day, may have to be abolished in a democracy; and the "virtues" which arise in poverty and war may have to be sacrificed, as well as those for which tuberculosis gives such splendid opportunities. To select among impulses is altogether good. Not all repression is therefore bad; and indeed, the art of life includes a skill in repression, which in common speech is "doing one thing at a time", or "concentrating upon the job in hand". The fact, however, that not all abilities are "in play" indicates a store of available ability in the common man, which may be used for contending with evil or for advancing what is good in the present situation. Therefore, even if the common man is proved to have been so far a failure in politics or economic activity or culture, it is much too soon to condemn the democratic ideal. The tendency to fear what is strange may have to be skilfully repressed, if men are to face a new social organization. Those who are accustomed to heavy clothing may have to repress the tendency to avoid the open air before being released from their burden; and nations may have to face the risks of peace before they lay down their arms. But with sufficient knowledge of facts and skill in the art of life, an immense store of new abilities may be released.

Again, in every large group, such as a nation, and even among the inhabitants of a city area, there are many sub-groups of men interested in or working together for this or that common factor in social life. The mental structure which unites those interested in dog-racing is quite distinct from that which unites those interested in music. And even in political issues, taken separately for the sake of argument, the "public opinion" on housing is the mental structure of the group of those who happen to be interested in that particular issue. It is very seldom that "public opinion" can be held to refer to the attitudes in a whole city area: still more seldom can it be made to refer to the attitudes in a whole nation. Opinions and attitudes spread more widely at crises; but there is always a nucleus of active interest in this or that subject and a surrounding protoplasm of susceptible minds. All the persons, however, to whom this statement applies may be common men, in the sense that, although interested in one subject rather than another, they are not exceptionally able or intelligent in reference to it. Thus, in any large community there are many "publics" having many different "opinions". But both these words are obsolete; for it is more correct to say that there are mind-groups with different "sets" or tendencies, which are formed of complexes and behaviour-patterns. The language of social theory cannot be changed by a suggestion or a decree; but clearly "will" is most misleading and all references to "opinion" displace what is now known about the motor-affective reactions by an altogether misleading individualistic intellectualism.

Finally, in all men is what distinguishes them from animals, their tendency to acquire new habits rapidly and permanently and in social groups. The important observation in this matter is, for example, that men now wear trousers and once wore togas. Similarly, they now use legs and arms for driving automobiles, unknown to their forefathers. To use the results of science does not make a man scientific; and an ape may drop bombs. But clearly some mental change has occurred in the tone of civilized life, as well as in the use of mechanisms. This, in psychological terms, indicates the permanence of that "idealistic impulse" which makes the common man susceptible to indications of a possible change for the better. And this impulse, connected with the so-called "exploratory" instinct, is far more important than contemporary habit; for it is the source of modifications of habit and therefore the basis of all reform. Without reference to this natural impulse, human history is unintelligible. It is as "natural" to man to depart from the habits of the anthropoid ape as it is "natural" for him to retain traces of his admirable ancestors.

All these factors underlie the existing structure of society, which contains both good and evil. The merely psychological analysis of the situation, however, does not indicate which impulse ought to be repressed and which more fully developed. Even the tendency to change is not necessarily a tendency in the right direction. But it has been shown in the last chapter that the two distinct directions now possible are towards democracy or towards dictatorship and that the democratic ideal allows for a freer play of more impulses, more intricately developed, than the authoritarian. This is assumed to be better, which obviously implies a conception of the good life not acceptable to all. Perhaps it is safer not to make implications too obvious, lest the argument be obscured by irrelevant controversies. But the good life implied as an ideal here is a full and varied energizing of all the abilities of each man which can be brought into play in good company. The ideal is Hellenic, not Hebraic; it is Dionysiac, not Apolline—if those old contrasts are valid. But its meaning can be understood only after an examination of actual social customs and institutions.

The general features of a community, which is affected by the democratic ideal, include elaborate organizations, associations, pulls, and stresses. We have ourselves inherited and adapted to new uses within the democratic tradition many institutions founded in pre-democratic days: and the older institutions feel the strain.[1] But further changes are necessary.

The problems to be considered, however, are not those of detail, such as a political party or an industrial board of directors may have to face. They are problems of general tendency, of principles underlying political action. Our task is not bricklaying but architecture. The design of the house, not the manipulations of the material for building it, must be dis-

[1] See Zimmern, *The Prospects of Democracy*.

cussed. And the house is to be designed for habitation, not to be viewed from outside. The institutions which we have inherited and now propose to modify are merely means for a certain kind of life. Most of them, however, were designed for kinds of life which we do not now desire, even if they were possible. An old-fashioned parliament, for example, may be quite good enough for a simple, mediæval homogeneous or largely agricultural society; but it may not be flexible enough for a rapidly changing heterogeneous, industrial life. An elementary school may be good enough to teach "lower classes" the three R's, but it may be useless in an egalitarian society for the full development of citizens. An industrial and financial system may be good enough for keeping a great number of "manual" workers always at work; but it may not produce enough leisure for the development of finer abilities. Again, most of our political institutions arose for redress of grievances and protection of the weak, but we have passed beyond the need for mere patchwork or charitable consideration. We desire progressive construction, not buttressing of old habits lest some new stress may destroy them. The first task of representative government was the destruction of privileges; and that has been very largely done. We need more. Modern government is organization for purposes quite unknown even in the early nineteenth century. But in all adaptations for the sake of a kind of life more civilized than ours to-day, there is one general feature which may be noted here. It is that the common man will have to play a greater part. That would make no situation better, if the common man were anything like what he is supposed to be by reactionaries and revolutionaries, or even like what it is implied he may be in the unguarded language of enthusiasts for democracy. If the common man is essentially a fool, or if he is merely an appetite for satisfactions, to give more power would destroy civilization. But he is neither. Language reveals assumptions, if the words are dissected. The tradition of political rhetoric includes the words "mass", "majority", "multitude"; and the word "people" or "public" is used to refer to an undifferentiated and innumerable group of men and women or of men only. But nothing at all is to be expected for civilization from the mass or the multitude; and it is a mistake for advocates of democracy to accept the terms as though democracy were mass-rule or rule by the multitude. The mistake is easily seen when the verbal transition is made from "mass" to "mob" and from "multitude" to "crowd", and mob-rule and the crowd-mind are taken to be phenomena of democracy. But that must be most strenuously denied to be valid. The abilities of the common man are left out of account in the traditional phrases.

The conceptions of the mass or the undifferentiated multitude, the mob and the crowd, are all due to persons who have little acquaintance with the common man. They are like the conceptions of sheep among those who are not shepherds and have no close contact with sheep. To these, one sheep is indistinguishable from another. So to the superior person all working-men are alike and all the people he sees in the street are just "the mass". A closer and more kindly inspection reveals important differences. What seemed to be "mass" is then seen to have a very highly developed structure. Within what seemed to be a mere crowd, different groupings appear; and democracy, as will be explained later, is the integration of these groups, not the dominance of a majority of atomic individuals.

It is not denied that mobs exist and in some places and at some times have control of policy. Nor is it denied that the mob-mind or the herd-mind or the crowd-mind is a phrase for an actual fact. The point is that to advocate democracy does not imply any approval of such facts. Indeed, the mob-mind or the herd-mind is much more likely to take control in an oligarchy than in a democracy; for when criticism is impossible and force is the chief instrument of authority, the lower elements of human ability are usually dominant.

And even when a finer mind uses the mob, the instrument eventually controls the hand that uses it. Certainly, some advocates of democracy have shown admiration for what is vulgar; and they have counted heads, irrespective of their contents. There have been demagogues among the democrats. The ideal, then, has been understood in senses quite different from that which is given to it here. But clearly both conceptions cannot be correct.

The meaning of the word democracy, however, cannot be discovered by counting the number of times it has been used in each of many senses. Its meaning is what is understood to be the main element in the situation to which it points, together with such other elements as are consistent with that. Many mistakes have been made by advocates of democracy: and some of the ends proposed as democratic have certainly not been so. It will appear, therefore, in the course of the argument that the democratic ideal implies the full vitality of the common man in good company and that conceptions irreconcilable with this imply defective thinking which may have to be corrected before the ideal itself can become more fully operative.

Psychologically stated, therefore, the ideal of democracy implies a community in which the natural differences between men are not diminished by their sociability. Their different emotional and intellectual abilities have freer play because conventional social barriers are lowered or abolished. The choice of occupation in such a society is decided not by reference to an arbitrary will of those who are rich, but by public policy based on the recognition of the needs of all members of the community. And the growth of new abilities, in perception of fact or skill, is the main purpose of education. But as the abilities and the vitality in action of the common man increase, more of the actual task of maintaining social institutions will fall to him. The result need not be an increased burden, if strength grows more rapidly than the new tasks are undertaken. And, indeed, a democratic ideal cannot be inculcated from above. It must arise among common men. Therefore, the further embodiment of that ideal, by a betterment of existing society, should occur, not as a result of unwilling and inevitable acceptance of public duties by common men, but as a result of their own vitality, demanding an outlet in a public service which is enjoyed because it brings new abilities into play.

CHAPTER III

GOVERNMENT AND THE COMMON MAN

POLITICAL institutions do not exist in a social vacuum. They are parts of a complex structure of social habits and tendencies, some of which are embodied in non-political institutions such as grocers' shops and schoolrooms. For the purpose of the argument, however, political institutions will be considered separately and will be held to include States, local authorities, civil services, parliaments, law courts, and the rest of that class. Undeniably they have become in modern times much more numerous and intricate. They affect the common man much more intimately; and in this section of social activities more than elsewhere the democratic ideal has operated. Indeed, democracy is sometimes taken to mean only a form of government. It is still unusual to speak of industrial democracy; and a democratic culture is still believed to be almost a contradiction in terms. But clearly democracy in political life cannot exist without a similar organization of industry and some general education. Therefore the political democracy with which the argument is here concerned, must be considered to be only one phase or aspect of that social ideal, which also affects industry and culture. The life of any community in its three aspects—political, economic, and cultural, is essentially one; but although the State is only one among many institutions, it is in recent history "central", and it has been so far the chief field for the increase of democratic liberties. What can the common man make of the State?

The forces available are to be stated in modern psychological terms. They are not merely so much "will" or "purpose"; nor so much reaction to the "sovereign guides, pleasure and pain". Every man is a complicated mental structure, forming part of a community with other such complicated minds. There are in each man dim impulses deep down, inherited atavistic tendencies, hidden complexes, sometimes suddenly operative in crises, and attractions towards all kinds of strange gods. No man is so completely one man as the simple psychology of "one man, one vote" seemed to imply. There are in some men distinguishable "personalities"—short of lunacy. There are rhythms in each life, with different "wave-lengths". There are innumerable unrealized possibilities of perception or emotion, apart from a certain range of developed capacities. And to take each man by himself is to simplify the facts; for no man is separable from the society to which he is said to belong, either in his thinking or his emotion. Language and emotional sympathy indicate how men think and feel together. Thus, the forces which make political life are violent but ordered, changeable but rhythmical: and all of them are forces uniting certain groups of men and dividing each group from others.

There are two tendencies among this tangle of forces which are important for the present argument. (1) The play of psychological factors produces a certain "set", direction, or current, which is maintained from day to day and gives form to the normal life of a community; and (2) these psychological factors bubble up from distinct centres either in what are called individual minds or in groups of minds. Any form of the life-current is called order: the bubbling-up is called liberty. A situation in which the established order promotes liberty is felt to be "just". Thus the current terms of political theory have their psychological implications; and the organization of any community is a natural growth in the mental life of the common man. The daily adjustment of each man to all the others in accepted custom, secured by law, is the State. Government is the system by which the adjustment is made; and there are two functions of government—deciding what to do, which is legislation, and seeing that it is done, which is administration. But the most important adjustment in normal times is administration, for most days are like the days before them, and most acts are habitual, even if the more significant acts are those done in a crisis or when a habit is not adequate to meet the needs of the situation. In any case, three-quarters of government is skill in administration; and legislatures are subordinate in importance most of the time for most men. Administration has always given to any particular form of government its dominant characteristics; and the development of political democracy is at least as much due to the organization and functioning of the public services as it is due to control by parliaments. Both the stability of a system of government and its flexibility can be traced to the methods used in the public services from the earliest times.

The history of democracy should not be regarded as simply a history of the legislature, but as also a history of the civil service. In the Middle Ages the English civil service developed a very great efficiency and a sense that they were servants of the nation, which was not obscured by their service in the King's household or the households of his high officials.[1] And by the accident of history in England the King's judges and the King's servants were not regarded as a caste opposed to the common folk; so that the *posse comitatus*, or body of sworn citizens, could be called upon to help the sheriffs to destroy the castles of oppressive or rebellious lords. Thus the police functions of the State were actually shared by common men—a very important factor in preventing the growth of opposition between governors and governed. Similarly the unprofessional Justices of the Peace and the jury system, using common men, whatever their defects, had the advantage of making acts of administration the acts of common men, and therefore bridging the gap between governing and being governed. The tradition of public service was not lost among the minor civil servants, even when corruption and nepotism were common among their superiors. And when the democratic

[1] See Tout, *Chapters in Mediæval Administration* and his pamphlet, *The English Civil Service in the Fourteenth Century.*

ideal in the nineteenth century affected representative legislatures, it also affected the choice of public servants.[1] When the nation came to be considered as the great majority and not the select few, the public service came also to be understood to mean service of this great majority.

It follows from this conception of the art of government that democracy cannot be established at one blow by the creation of a representative legislature. A public service with a democratic connection among common men is essential to the efficacy of the democratic ideal in politics. But the early history of the Civil Service is less important for the present argument than the recent change in its functions; for police, civil and criminal law, and defence are no longer the most significant activities of the State, if the meaning of political democracy is in question.

In the history of government a great transformation took place about seventy years ago. The process is not yet complete; but, in its most general character, it is nothing less than a change from the authoritarian State to the State as a public service. The contrast does not imply that the older form of State was not a form of service; but, first, the King and the King's servants, in the days when "sovereignty" seemed the most important aspect of their position, did not generally conceive themselves to be at the beck and call of the common man. If they served him, it was at their will and with their conception of what was good for him. The method of service was that in which the parent serves the child; and Government implied the principle of benevolence, not of rights and justice. And secondly, such service as was rendered to the common man, by the maintenance of the King's peace or the King's justice, was generally conceived as service of a superior, not service of the road-mender, the charwoman, the shoemaker, the smith, as well as service of the trader and the landowner.

[1] See H. Finer, *The Civil Service*, and my article in the *Encyclopædia Britannica*, Supplementary Volumes, 1926, on "Civil Services".

Just as the "people" were supposed to be "represented" in Great Britain by the absurd franchises of 1832 or 1867—just as the "people" are supposed now to be represented in France, although half of them, namely, the women, are not counted—so the State services of earlier times were not conceived as if "the public" included the majority of living men, women, and children. The transformation which has occurred in the last seventy years has made State activities into services of the common man.

The character of pre-modern government is indicated best by the functions performed by public servants. There were in all States, before about 1850, defence departments and police departments, but no departments of health, education, or even commerce. Soldiers and naval men gave the most prominent form of public service, and the law was either a statement of rights or a prohibition of evil acts, with sanctions or penalties attached. Thus, government was the art of control or keeping order by the methods of the most obsolete schoolmaster, *plagosus Orbilius*. The chief political experience of the common man was being dominated by Authorities.

In the middle years of the nineteenth century the democratic ideal began to affect administration, partly because the city areas had come into existence and the newly crowded populations discovered common needs of sanitation. This occurred in all Western countries. The theory of the eighteenth-century revolution in thought was confirmed by the experience of industrial revolution in the early nineteenth century; and men in power found that they could not neglect the interests of those who had no power. The process by which government changed its character was gradual; and a beginning of the change can be traced even in the eighteenth century. But the most striking changes have occurred within the past seventy years. The functions of the State and the nature of government have changed in all countries which have fallen under the influence of the democratic ideal.

The history of British administration may be taken as typical. First came the increase of public administration in regard to economic activities, trade, and manufacture. From very early times the State had provided the currency on which economic exchange depended; and not even the most obsolete individualist now regards the provision of a currency as "interference" by government. But it was found, when exchange of goods and services expanded beyond the mediæval range, that security of expectation, which was required for life and limb, had to be organized also with regard to economic relations. Laws of property and contract were followed by laws in regard to joint-stock companies and foreign commerce; and the new system was maintained by an "economic" department—the Board of Trade. Then "labour" or "employment" became a problem of economic policy; and the Trade Boards and Labour Statistics Departments were added to the Board of Trade. Conciliation and arbitration of industrial disputes were then added to the functions of government; and finally, in 1917, a new Ministry of Labour was established to carry on the non-commercial work hitherto done by the Board of Trade. In the promotion of what was regarded as an "essential" industry, the Department of Agriculture and Fisheries was set up. The development was rapid. The transformation of government took place in less than fifty years; but it is still not commonly understood that the State is not what it was in the early nineteenth century. There were hardly any functions of the State at that date corresponding to the many activities now exercised through "economic" departments.

Meantime, the old law and police department, the Home Office, had attached to it in 1833 a Factory Inspectors' Department, because the new Factory Acts were conceived as methods of preventing "wrongs". The early factory inspectors were catchers of criminals and therefore a form of police. That conception is now obsolete; but, for our argument here, what is important is that the State in the 1830's began to regulate methods of production.[1] The Factory Department is still attached to the law and police department, the Home Office; but its function is now co-operation, not control, in so far as it assists the organizers of industry to make labour more efficient. The protection of workers is now generally recognized to be for the advantage, not only of the workers, but also of the employers and of the public served. In this respect the State is not merely a police power. Again, the new sanitary legislation of the 1830's, under the inspiration of Chadwick, led to new functions of "Local Authorities"—which are quite obviously not Authorities in the old sense, but Services—and to the formation of the Local Government Board. This was combined with the Health Services of the Central Government, set up in 1911, to form in 1917 the Ministry of Health. The State has, therefore, entered into a field quite unknown even to Hegel's Absolute in the early nineteenth century. It is assisting daily in the development of the physical health of the comman man. The result has been startling. In 1850 the annual death-rate for England and Wales was 19·9; in 1922 it was 12·8 of every 1,000. In 1850 the infantile mortality was 146; in 1922 it was 77 of every 1,000 births. The average expectation of life at birth has increased by over ten years, and "there is no inherent reason why as much as three years should not be added to the average life of Englishmen of 45".[2] In terms of vitality and happiness, the improvement of the last fifty years in the life of the common man is one of the best arguments for the democratic ideal. Its operation means not only longer life for common folk, but more energy during life, owing to the elimination of disease. And this has been done through the State.

Finally, government in the later nineteenth century began

[1] See below, p. 154, for government and industry in their present relation.

[2] See Robson, *Relation of Wealth to Welfare*, where the words are quoted from the Report of the Chief Medical Officer, 1921, p. 21.

to provide funds and organization for education. The State took over the timid beginnings made by "the Church" and immensely extended education, both with regard to the numbers provided for and with regard to the subjects and methods of education. Again, here is a service quite unknown to the traditional political philosophy. New departments and new types of public service had to be created; and the creation took place in most Western countries simultaneously within the memory of men now living. The State is no longer a form of authority in the old sense. It is an organization for the benefit of common men; and its excellences or its defects are judged by reference to the value of the benefits they receive or by its ability to increase those benefits.

Changes in legislative power reflect the same transformation of the State. The British Parliament is no longer mainly concerned with laws enacting or maintaining rights, nor with laws forbidding wrongs. Its time is devoted mainly to (1) the creation of new organizations for public services, and to (2) adjustments of the action of citizens with respect to these organizations. That is to say, the State is being made into a complete system of public service, and "authority" is coming to mean only the influence of expert knowedge or of common agreement. Similar changes in the work of legislatures occurred at the same time in all Western countries; but legislation will be discussed later. The section of the art of government which is day-to-day administration must now be considered as a whole.

The increase of services implies a greater energy devoted to the common good. More of a modern man's "good" is social than was the case in the Middle Ages; for our social contacts are more numerous, more varied, and more continuous. This is largely the result of economic changes and the social gravitation which has produced large city areas. But whatever the cause, the functions of government have changed.[1] The relation,

[1] There is in Aristotle's *Politics* a recognition of the diverse relationship

therefore, between governing and being governed is now quite different from what it was in earlier times and that, partly at any rate, because of the operation of the democratic ideal. Most of the old books on democracy are obsolete. Most of the theories of government do not allow for the recent change in its character. But the argument here is concerned only with this one aspect of the question—what is the present position of the common man with regard to officials or public servants?

We pass, therefore, from the analysis of the facts to an interpretation of the necessities of the situation. In order that the democratic ideal may become still more fully operative, certain habits and customs of the common man and his servants will have to be changed. The State is not what it ought to be, if one considers the present waste in disease, ignorance, or incompetence. If we are to go farther in the direction recently followed, institutions may have to be changed; but above all, certain inherited habits and tendencies must be transformed. First, the official public servant must be no longer aloof, superior, dictatorial, or dilatory—that is to say, setting his own pace. Secondly, the common man must form part of the administrative machine in daily acts. In other terms, if in a democracy all government is for the sake of the people, in the sense that it is a service of common men in their daily needs, then governing and being governed are no longer functions of two distinct classes. The official must be amenable to social influences; and the society in which he acts must provide for him assistance and friendliness. Indeed, the significant difference between a democratic and a non-democratic society is to be found in the attitude of the common man towards the police and other servants of the State. When they are regarded with friendliness, the situation is democratic: when they are suspected or feared, autocracy of some kind survives.

of citizens, needing governmental organization, which reads as if it were a list of modern government offices. But obviously Aristotle is thinking in terms which ignore the modern distinction between the State and non-governmental institutions within any community.

But in actual experience in any large community some groups still fear and suspect public servants and some public servants are still despots.

First, therefore, the attitude and conduct of officials must change; but there are already signs of change. It will be shown below that methods of inspection of factories, for example, or schools, have changed. The inspector in many cases is not a police agent for hounding down law-breakers, but an assistant in an enterprise. And further, outside that function of administration called inspection, there is a change; for officials cannot act in employment exchanges or education or health offices as they act in police measures against crime, and even policing is now very largely a direction of traffic rather than a catching of criminals.

Again, great numbers of officials are distributors of benefits, such as pensions, insurance funds, compensation, or donations for the necessitous. In primitive minds this "public assistance" still appears to be regrettable; and clearly the occasion for it is regrettable. But there is no possible doubt that most public assistance is not a mere superfluous benevolence at the expense of the public purse. It is generally a grant of rights or of what is due to certain servants of the public, injured or aged in the rendering of service. This is apart altogether from the necessary support of lunatics or helpless cripples, who must be a public charge in any real community. Again, the modern State has set up offices for the adjustment of industrial disputes and appointed officials to conciliate or to forestall such disputes, whose contacts with employers and trade unionists are by no means the contacts of superiors with their inferiors. The "power" of an official in such matters is negligible: his competence in influencing men is of the greatest importance. Thus authority comes to mean competence, not status: and the power of the State means only a sphere for the performance of a function.

The technique of administration in the new services must

be different from the old-fashioned command or direction from above; and the new technique is actually practised in any good employment exchange or pensions office. In the book of instructions for tax-collectors in Great Britain, issued in 1911 and re-issued in 1916, it is said: "Every person having recourse to a Surveyor's office on business is entitled to all necessary advice and assistance without charge." Again, in June 1928, the instructions to the civil servants of the department were as follows:

> The general attitude of the Department should be one of readiness to assist the taxpayer in every reasonable way. Accordingly, the Board desire that their officers should at all times, as far as may be practicable (1) Draw the attention of taxpayers to any reliefs to which they appear to be clearly entitled but which they may have omitted to claim, including, where applicable, the consequential effect of any relief allowable for Income Tax purposes upon Super-Tax liability, and (2) Respond freely to any requests that may be made by taxpayers for advice as to their rights and liabilities or for guidance in formulating claims to relief.

Although the new democratic attitude and technique are being developed, the change has not yet been completed. Some officials inherit not only obsolete forms of action, but obsolete manners and customs. Thus the "Jack in office", the insolent controller of the public life of others, is not unknown. But, worse still, besides survivals there are revivals of the obsolete. For example, the police in many parts of Great Britain adopt an obsolete attitude towards those whose servants they are. The Police Commission recently in session in London has revealed by accident some dangerous tendencies to tyranny. The Chief Constable of Birmingham, giving evidence before the Commission, is reported to have said:[1] "There seems to be an idea that the poorer classes know less about criminal law than the more educated. That is not the case. The criminal classes and their associates know criminal law extremely well." This probably accidental identification

[1] *Manchester Guardian*, November 16, 1928.

of crime with poverty reflects the obsolete assumptions from which some public officials still suffer.

Again, one of the police witnesses before the same Commission is reported to have complained of "the growing truculence of the public",[1] exactly as if a cook should complain of the truculence of those who pay her in refusing to eat boiled potatoes. The authoritarian State evidently survives among the police, although they have in the modern State no power or function at all, except as servants of the common man.[2] On the other hand, the Chief Constable of Glasgow, writing in the *Glasgow Herald* on December 15, 1928, although he slips into an unfortunate phrase about "the control of pedestrians", does appreciate the new situation when he says: "If in busy centres pedestrians would, so far as they can, avoid crossing streets except at crossings when traffic is stopped, it would greatly assist in reducing the causes of accidents and facilitate the progress of vehicular traffic." It is interesting to hear the pedestrian called upon to assist the motorist, presumably on the understanding that the motorist will not regard the pedestrian on a road as legitimate prey. But the new functions of the common man will be discussed later. It is enough for the moment to note the difference between the old and the new conception of public authority and public service.

A striking change, also quite recent, in bridging the gap between the old-fashioned governing and being governed is the creation in Great Britain of Local Authorities under the Municipal Corporations Act, 1882, and the Local Government Act, 1888. As a result of these Acts administration is carried on by elected representatives. Thus the Report on the Ceylon Constitution, proposing a form of government

[1] *Manchester Guardian*, November 21, 1928.

[2] It is assumed that the police are not merely protectors of the beneficiaries of a social system against its victims: but that assumption is evidently not accepted by some "educated classes", as may be seen in the collection raised for the police through the columns of the London *Times* after the Stoppage of 1926.

similar to that in British Local Authorities, gives as a reason for the proposal that "it is a scheme which is calculated to divert attention from the academic discussion of political theory to the practical consideration of the pressing administrative problems of to-day".[1] Elected administrators may be bad at administration, and local government officials should be chosen by tests of competence, not by personal "influences"; but the important point for our argument is that in practice the gap between governors and governed is decreased in countries affected by the democratic ideal.[2] It is to be hoped that the argument will not be misunderstood; but the chances are that it will. Some will quote instances of official dilatoriness or of insolent authoritarianism. Clearly the new technique is not everywhere practised. The argument rests only on (1) the existence of some officials who are of a new kind, and on (2) the evident conclusion that, if State services are public services of common men, officials must be friendly assistants and not dictators. The operation of the democratic ideal in the past fifty years has in fact dissolved the hard crust of the official caste and therefore diminished bureaucracy. But the ideal is not by any means achieved, and for its further progress great improvements are necessary in the manners and customs of officials. It is therefore to be hoped that the Institute of Public Administration, in the pursuit of efficiency in the public services, will not omit to note the importance of manners.[3]

The extension of public services which the transformation of government has entailed is still resisted by many. It is said that democracy causes "bureaucracy". Some, in the old Spencerian tradition, mean by bureaucracy, not the bad manners of officialdom, but the fact that the number of officials

[1] See Report Cmd. 3131, 1928, p. 46.

[2] For difficulties of local incompetence see *Royal Commission on Local Government* evidence of Graham Wallas and W. A. Robson, March 1, 1928.

[3] The bluster and violence of Fascist officials in Italy, which is destroying the traditional *gentilezza*, well known to lovers of the old Italy, is a sign of anti-democratic ideals. This is a more important sign than the mere absence of elected legislatures.

is large. If, however, officials are public servants and we are the public, it is hardly reasonable to object to having more servants to look after our interests. Clearly a great number of servants may be superfluous in any household; but it is not to be assumed that the past, when the public needs were simpler, sets the standard. Nor can it be reasonably regarded as an economy to deprive ourselves of services which would increase the general health or vitality. Indeed, the cry for "economy" in public services, which means fewer civil servants or lower payments to them, generally comes from those whose sense of the community is so weak that they cannot reckon as gain anything which is not an asset in their private banking accounts. There are many who claim to be educated, who are quite ignorant of the services performed for their sake by the State in the decrease of infectious disease and the increase of daily supplies of water, drainage and roads.

Apart, however, from minor objections to an increase in the number of public servants, there are two great dangers in the modern practices by which the efficiency of the public services has been increased. It is obviously good that the administration should be powerful and secure; but the practice of delegated legislation, Statutory Orders in Great Britain, and similar procedure abroad, leads to rules being framed without the criticism of those whom they most nearly affect. And, secondly, the growth of administrative law or special rules and procedure for the advantage of the administration in any dispute with the citizen has reached alarming proportions even in Great Britain.[1]

Legislation will be discussed below; but clearly in a democracy even delegated rule-making should be affected by the opinions of those whom the rules closely affect, since all law in a democratic community implies an agreement as to action

[1] See W. A. Robson, *Justice and Administrative Law*, and Port, *Administrative Law*; and for Statutory Orders see my *Government and Industry*.

to be taken by each citizen. Therefore the rule-making of officials should be under constant supervision of special committees of competent persons; and the democratization of administrative methods therefore involves not merely a change in character or conduct, but a reform of institutions.[1] The new departments of public service are by no means perfect; and the next steps in democracy may very well be some improvement in the machinery of government. But the argument here is not concerned with the details necessary for such a policy. The principles of personal action are no less important for the democratic ideal.

There is one section in the practice of administration which has hardly at all been affected by the changes in the functions and methods of modern government. The growth of a democratic administration in which the official is in practice a servant of the common man and the common man a coadjutor in governing does not in practice affect the government of subject or undeveloped peoples. Colonial government is seldom considered by political theorists; and advocates of democracy apply its principles fantastically to primitive tribes when they say that "one man, one vote" is a method applicable to them. The whole problem needs examination; but here it is enough to suggest certain general principles consonant with the modern view of government.[2]

First, the problem is administrative, not that of representative legislatures in the old theory. Secondly, the solution lies in decreasing the gap between governors and governed, which implies a new attitude and new conduct on both sides. Government is not merely a police system, but is an instrument of public health, education, and economic development for the sake of all the governed, and not in order to make

[1] The suggestions made by H. J. Laski in his *Grammar of Politics* are implied here.

[2] These principles are very clearly expressed in the *Report of the Commission on Eastern Africa*, Cmd. 3234, 1929. See also *Ceylon: Report on Constitution*, Cmd. 3131, 1928.

some of them efficient instruments of the fortunes of the others; but because the majority in an undeveloped population have no means of understanding the resources of modern administration or the contacts with the outer world which the new functions of government necessitate, the control of the administration must be in the hands of the citizens of the State under whose jurisdiction the undeveloped population lives. Those who appoint the officials and support them must bear the moral responsibility for their service of the governed until the governed are able not only to be "represented", but to assist in the daily administration. Democratic government, therefore, in some modern States, involves trusteeship for native populations, for the sole purpose of developing democratic methods of government in those populations.

Finally, the way in which the native population should be developed must depend upon their own customs and traditions; and it is by no means certain that in every case voting for representatives and jury-systems are the best methods of increasing the abilities of common men in public affairs. The democratic ideal may be effectual through other means than those which arose out of social conditions in Great Britain. In order to increase native ability at once administrative changes may be necessary; but the further discussion of democratic principles in reference to colonial government must be omitted, since the advance of democracy within a governing people must probably precede the application of democracy in the government of subject races.

Far more important than administrative changes or changes in the manner of officials is the change in the common man's attitude and action, which is necessary for the increase of democracy. It is futile to imagine the civil service as a hidden and sinister power, likely to entrap the honest citizen or to hinder his pursuit of his business. If public servants are tyrants or thieves, no institutions are adequate to protect the common man. But, in any case, the best way to secure a more competent public service is to produce more competent citizenship among common men; and it is precisely here that the abilities of the common man are in doubt. Can he cease to regard himself as a sheep driven by government and come to act as an intelligent co-operator in governing?

Obviously, as social life becomes more complicated, the individual has greater responsibility. Even in early times in the British tradition the common man could be summoned at any time to assist the public authorities. And the responsibility for helping the police when they are in need is still enforced upon the citizen in British Common Law, although the King's peace is not now so often in jeopardy as it was in the Middle Ages.

In service under arms in the recent war it was recognized that the soldier, and still more the airman, often had to act as an individual on his own judgment and without waiting for orders. The complexity and extent of modern operations makes it impossible to treat even the soldier as a merely passive tool for the commander. Still more obviously in the less barbaric enterprises of peace the individual citizen cannot be left to be ordered by authority. In modern traffic the driver of an automobile has to contribute some understanding and skill of his own, if police regulation is to be effectual. The pedestrian must know the regulations for his own safety and himself assist in their maintenance. It is calculated that 83 per cent. of street accidents in Great Britain in 1928 were due to errors of judgment on the part of pedestrians, cyclists, and motorists; and from 1918 to 1928, 40,000 deaths in Great Britain have been due to road accidents. The Safety First Association pleads for "the education of all road users;"[1] and obviously the education suggested is some training in the individual's contribution to order in this matter. Similarly, the system of State education implies the need for co-operation

[1] Pamphlet issued in 1928.

on the part of parents, sending their children to school, or taking them to the dentist or oculist, when advised to do so by the medical officer. Again, in the maintenance of the conditions of health the public authority may provide the drains, but the individual has his part to play in the avoidance of spitting and other dangerous practices. Thus the change in the character of government involves an entry of the common man into the ranks of public servants in so far as he must assist in governing.

It is unnecessary to point out that the punctual payment of rates and taxes, the observance of the rule of the road, the supervision over the cleanliness and security of the premises used, are all parts of the active contribution of citizens to the administration, and that under a democracy they would not depend merely upon the efficacy of penalties against those who may avoid their duties. In addition, new laws, such as that of National Health Insurance, involve the citizen in the stamping of cards; and non-State organizations such as Trade Unions assist in the performance of administrative functions. But, most striking of all, the old unpaid and untrained magistracy of the Justices of the Peace in Great Britain has been extended to include men and women of all social classes. The jury system has been made to include women. And in the creation since 1882 and 1888 of Local Authorities common men elect not merely representative legislatures but administrations. The councillor acts not only as a maker of rules, but as a director of policy in social services; and by co-option for such purposes as education persons specially competent in this or that subject are given power over the daily acts of government.

The chief point of the argument is that, as the services of the State are more highly organized, the citizens concerned necessarily play a more important part in the maintenance of the organization. This, and not merely voting at elections, is government by the people; for in this more than in legislation self-government is a reality and governing rather than being governed becomes a normal function of the citizen. Thus, government becomes, in the normal assumptions of common life and not merely in theory, a public service, not only because every man is served by it, but also because every man has some part to play in that service. It is no longer, then, possible for the citizens of a democratic State to regard government as the function of some body of men alien to them or having interests other than theirs. A new art of government is being developed by comparison with which the authoritarian methods of the past are primitive.

But the future is by no means certain. The democratic organization of political society has its dangers, because the common man, whose co-operation is essential for its success, may be incompetent or unwilling to co-operate. The alternative system of organization is regimentation, which is now advocated as a new idea by Fascists and Communists. Making people do what they ought and doing for them the thinking required, is like ready-reckoning from a list of prepared calculations; but it is believed by dictators to be a method of avoiding the danger that the common man may be incompetent or unwilling.

The argument, however, against such methods as systems of government is that they cause more incompetence and unwillingness than already exists. A man used as a mere instrument of another will becomes a mere instrument; and thus most of his human ability is lost. The most fatal argument against all forms of tyranny is not the cruelty of the tyrant, but the inertia and apathy of his subjects. But now that government is no longer so simple as it was, the authoritarian method is obsolete; for health services and education, not to speak of modern systems of production and transport, cannot be maintained by automata. Other purposes may be attained by Fascism and Communism, but not the purposes of the modern State.

It follows that democracy has a great advantage in the risk it involves. The risk of a lack of public spirit in a democracy is more than compensated by the opportunities for the exercise of such public spirit as exists; for by the exercise of even a little public spirit the common man develops more. It has been proved by the results of public health and educational organization that abilities existed which were not available until such organisation was introduced; and this is a basis for the legitimate hypothesis that even more abilities may be found in the common man than are now in play.

Existing political institutions in countries where the democratic tradition is established do not yet give enough place to the common man. The complaint that there is a lack of public spirit is often unwise; and the attempt to correct the deficiency by exhortations to citizenship is too simple-minded. Most exhortation is futile. It ends not in doing good but in feeling good; and when a man feels good he is probably at his worst. But doing what ought to be done can be directly promoted by institutions which give scope for action. There is no need to pump energy into the common man. He has quite enough; but it is repressed by custom, belief, and superior persons. To free him from such repression is the purpose of all education; and education includes every method by which a man learns to do more than he has already done.

If a modern argument may be summarized in a mediæval syllogism—all government is a method of education; but the best education is self-education; therefore the best government is self-government, which is democracy.

CHAPTER IV

REPRESENTATIVES AND LAW

THE advocates of what was called democracy in the nineteenth century aimed chiefly at the control of government by means of voting on the part of larger groups of men for representatives in legislative assemblies. Government was conceived in terms of authority; and law-making was believed to be its chief function. Thus by a series of accidents, and as a result of conclusions drawn from very inadequate evidence, the decision as to who shall make laws and what laws shall be made was held to rest ultimately with those who voted for representatives. Metaphors were freely used to show that this was self-government; and it was generally assumed that those who had a vote were "the people", even if they were only a small group of male householders. The logical result, however, in those countries which are said to be less logical than France has been that women also and all other sane adults now have the vote.

But precisely here the question as to the abilities of the common man becomes most urgent. He may be able to assist the police and to pay taxes willingly; but is he capable of deciding on policy in a crisis, or even of choosing a person to speak for him who is competent to decide?

The answer to such questions must depend upon what representation and legislation are; and it must not be assumed that the traditional views of them are correct. The supposed failure of democracy or the incompetence of the common man, in the view of the opponents of democracy, may be due to a mistake either as to what is actually happening or as to what should happen. For example, as it has been shown above, to say that the common man is incompetent in his choice because a scholar does not like the sort of person he chooses may only prove that tastes differ; and the scholar is often a bad judge of the competence required in politics. Or, again, the incompetence of democracy may be only the inability of a new form of government to preserve the privileges natural in an older form, and the loss of such privileges may be good. The test of success is not generally made by the opponents of democracy in terms of health and peace. First, then, what actually happens? What are the factors in political life which representatives represent?

The life of society is largely habitual. The common man and the genius or the fool, in so far as the common man is in him, are most of the time concerned with action, attitudes, and thought, which do not vary from day to day. But no man's habits would "run" unless they fitted into the habits of those with whom each is in contact. This fitting of the behaviour of one man into the behaviour of others so as to make a social pattern is not normally the result of intellectual calculation as to how other men are likely to act. But it is not "blind"; nor is there any natural force or "hidden hand" which fits men's behaviour-patterns into a social life; nor is it safe to call its cause "instinct" because of the ambiguities of that word. It is due in each man to intelligent perception and motor-affective reaction in the presence of other men; and the most important point for the argument here is that this sensitiveness to social atmosphere is one of the greatest abilities of the common man. The genius in mathematics or in economics is often insensitive socially. The common man feels his connections with his fellows. He reacts easily to an appeal for help or sympathy. His understanding, which is restricted in regard to abstract problems, is keen enough in regard to practical issues. He may not know anything about the functions of a complex variable; but he knows well enough the distinction between a fool and a wise man, even if the fool is called a professor and the wise man a dustman.

Why should this amiable tendency to good fellowship be called abusively the herd instinct? Even wolves are insulted by what is implied in such a phrase; but our modern psychologists look backward. They trace origins, not ends. The association of men in groups may have some connection with the herding of animals; but even if its origin is discovered, that discovery cannot explain why the first stage in evolution has been left so far behind. Again, the phrases "mob mind" or "crowd mind" are often used to refer to the social cohesiveness of groups in which each man is sensitive to what the others are feeling. But such cohesiveness is not only normal; it is also excellent for political co-operation. It implies a recognition of the fact that no man thinks or feels alone. In each man are his ancestors; round him are his friends. Every man fits with *some* other men and not with all and sundry. And it is this social life which is to be "represented" in bringing to bear upon public policy the contributions of the common man. Thus, voting for representatives is not normally the result of individual calculation of interests, based on individual analysis of evidence. It is largely the result of "pulls" and attractions and half-conscious tendencies shared with other men. Clearly one man with great influence really votes many times, if many other men vote under his influence. But that is not objectionable unless the kind of influence so used is objectionable. The old-fashioned democracy of "one man, one vote" treated each man as a segregate unit; and the absurd results are now urged as objections to democracy itself. But democracy does not imply the denial of facts in normal social life; and if men are not calculating machines, to say that the social band is emotional or motor-affective is not to degrade it. The purpose of voting is not to collect "opinions", but to show how many can or will *work together*. What is to be represented in a democracy is the actual co-operation or willingness to co-operate of men who live in groups, intellectually and emotionally. What particular groups are suitable for representation is a secondary problem; but first the nature of the representative should be considered.

The representative does not represent men taken singly. He

or she is to "speak for" the social sympathy of an effectual group; and therefore a special kind of competence is required in the political representative. He must have or must be given some special ability to grasp a social atmosphere. He must react to what is sometimes called group-consciousness; and he must not be one of those who are naturally aloof or isolated in abstraction. It is unlikely that a good scientist will be a good representative. Again, the representative should have the power to state—what perhaps no one of his constituents could state so well—the purposes implied in a group-consciousness which is seldom deliberately purposive; and in such a statement he confirms, strengthens, and even forms, almost out of nothing, a new stage in the group-consciousness. That is to say, representation in one respect is interpretation of the mental structure of a community.

Again, the representative must be intelligible. It is fortunate if he is also intelligent; but intelligible he must be. A very excellent logical proof may be useless as a means of persuasion; and persuasion is the function of the representative. This does not imply that he should neglect logic for rhetoric, because after all the best rhetoric is logical; but he should not neglect the fact that in politics the instrument is man, and the force to move men from within is persuasion. His preparation of that instrument by making himself intelligible to the common man in an election should be followed by a use of the instrument in the interval between elections. One of the functions of the representative after election, therefore, is to explain to his constituents the view of public good which is obtained from the central position to which he has been appointed; and it is not democracy if a representative, once elected, never consults his constituents. All representatives, like public officials, are agents. The method of selecting them by voting rather than by competitive examination seems to aim at discovering who is intelligible, not who is intelligent. But it is foolish to underrate intelligibility. Einstein has other excellences. It requires great skill and subtlety, not merely to tell the truth, but to make others see that it is the truth. Thus, when the representatives come together in a Council or Parliament they speak what most men are able to see to be the truth; and in that sense the representative system is a means whereby the common man is called into consultation for government.

The old argument for representation seemed to imply, as Rousseau certainly believed, that this was an unfortunate necessity. It was believed that, only because there were too many of them, were common men compelled to use representatives. This conception, however, rests on the old individualism. The real reason for the representative system is not that we can find space only for a few to consult together, but that only a few are likely to have the competence to "speak for" a group-consciousness. It is essential to social action, and not an unfortunate necessity, that the separate individual citizens of a State should *not* be in consultation; for it is likely that only a few have more than the vaguest sense of the common good. Representation requires skill in perceptiveness and in expression, of which the majority in any community are not capable; and that kind of skill is wasted or swamped in general assemblies of all members of a community. It follows that the so-called direct democracy of the Athenian ecclesia and of Swiss cantons is not such good democracy as representation provides.

If that is representation, what groups ought to be represented in a democracy? In general each group that has a unity of co-operation between its members, which implies, not necessarily identity of opinion, but willingness of one to work with another. Agreement in general policy is usually a sign of willingness to co-operate; but it cannot be too often asserted that government is action, not opinion. The best proof of willingness to work together is that men actually do work together as neighbours, or as following the same trade. But because the issues generally faced in public policy affect men rather as neighbours than as workers in this or that trade, therefore the groups which develop representation of themselves are territorial. And because future action for the common good usually depends much more on what one's neighbours do than upon what one's fellow-worker does, therefore the disagreements as to what future action should be taken are disagreements between neighbours, not between men in different trades or within the same trade.[1] The progress of the democratic ideal so far has led to a voting power held by all sane adults, men and women; and the mental structure of any community is reflected in the groupings which are actually represented in legislative assemblies. But the fundamental change in extending the franchise to all adults has been made only within the past ten years in most countries; and the mental structures resulting from the use of the new power have hardly yet begun to form. Representatives still live on the platitudes of the eighteenth century; and the methods of connecting these public servants with the persons served are still primitive. Canvassing is probably in most cases ridiculous; and the test of competence in a candidate very crude.[2] But new devices are being tried—the cinema, the wireless, for example; and the technique of representation will therefore probably change. The only conclusion which can be made in these early days of a great experiment is that new abilities of the common man will undoubtedly come into play now that women and youths contribute to the common store of judgment on public affairs.

In the democratic tradition two incidental methods are used for bringing the common man into more continuous and intimate touch with affairs than could be achieved by voting at elections: one is the free political association in diverse or opposing parties,

[1] It will be understood that "functional representation" in political legislatures is being opposed in what is stated here. But if the structure of society changes, functional representation may become useful. It is used in a very limited sense now under cover of territorial divisions, as when coal districts elect miners or agents of companies sit for suburbia.

[2] See George Meredith's *Beauchamp's Career*.

the other is a free Press. These are as essential to democracy as the representative system. A political party is a group of persons acting together for certain consciously accepted purposes; but the group is a real mental unity of many minds, not a mere collection of individuals. In any party there is an active nucleus of enthusiasts and a surrounding protoplasm of sympathizers. The party organisers aim at selecting competent candidates to offer themselves as possible representatives, and at mobilizing the support necessary for this or that candidate. The party thus educates its sympathizers and attempts to influence others; and already much has been achieved since the days when parties were merely gangs of rival vultures hovering over the public purse.

But the parties of to-day are still under the influence of theological controversy. They are normally groups of men entirely blind to anything but sacred phrases of their own; and it may not yet be possible for men to act decidedly without dogmatic beliefs. Thus party controversy is often like the old theological disagreements in which each side assumed that it had the truth and that all it needed was evidence to support a case already decided. The peculiar habit of advocacy in the practice of the law reinforces the bad habit of adopting a case before deciding what the evidence proves. Thus argument takes the place of reasoning; for in reasoning the conclusion is not known until the premises have been used, but any man who already "knows" the truth can only look for confirmation of it, not for evidence against it. Dogma, in the traditional sense, is an obstacle to democratic processes in politics.

But political parties obviously differ in character in different countries because of different social habits or different political institutions. For example, if general elections are held at fixed periods, as in the French method, every four years, then parties tend to be groups of elected representatives, not groups of constituents; for in the interval between general elections disagreements between the constituents are irrelevant. Again, if the Chamber is so constructed that a tribune for the orator faces equally all parties, the orator tends to use the rhetoric of the platform, not the conversational argument of a committee. The mere structure of a Chamber thus makes a psychological difference; and the British House of Commons can easily be compared in this matter with the Reichstag or the French Chamber of Deputies. Similarly, the forms of business differ in the London County Council and the Glasgow City Corporation; and this affects the character of representation through parties.

The free Press, the other great means of contact between the common man and public affairs, is a modern invention. The influence of the existing newspapers has never been analysed psychologically, although the defects of the Press have been exposed.[1] Platitudes fill the air, both in praise and condemnation of journalists; but for the argument here a note is sufficient. Some journalists accept the responsibility which their power implies; others quite cheerfully are reckless, and by their efforts to sell any news increase the scepticism of common men as to all news. The most important factor in present experience is the widespread distrust of all "official" news, which has been the result of official communiqués and propaganda during the war.[2] Similarly, the power of small groups of wealthy men in the control of the Press is probably not so great as they would like to believe that it is. The progress of democracy probably depends upon the increase of scepticism in the common man; but only if scepticism as to rumour does not corrode the ability to act. It was said of a certain politician that he did not know how far he went, but he knew that he did not go too far. That is reaction. The principle of democratic policy is rather that other, given by Henry James, namely, that one can never be certain that one has gone far enough until it is clear that one has gone too far.[3] A free Press at least may increase the number of possible beliefs and policies.

[1] See Arthur Ponsonby, *Falsehood in War Time*, and C. E. Playne, *The Neuroses of the Nations* and *The Pre-War Mind in Britain.*

[2] See Jean de Pierrefeu, *Plutarque a menti.* [3] Nash, in *The Tragic Muse*

In communities influenced by the democratic tradition the actual persons in power are chosen by a majority of voters; and in the assemblies the policy followed is decided by a majority. What is the moral ground for acceptance of such majority rule? Clearly it is not a moral ground that the majority have more physical power, even if they have, which is doubtful. Sometimes it is said that the majority are likely to be right because "two heads are better than one"; but minorities are often superior in judgment to majorities, and in any case it is ridiculous to suppose that fifty-one people out of an hundred are wiser than forty-nine. Where the majority is "narrow" the moral ground for accepting their guidance would be weak, if it were merely a probability of their being right that made all men accept their decision. The old arguments intended to explain the undoubted utility of majority rule are inadequate if not actually mistaken, for they rest on the false arithmetic of added "opinions".

A quite different ground for majority rule can be discovered, if the conception of government as daily action is understood; for then the majority is simply the largest number *willing to work together* for a particular purpose. Thus government by majority methods is simply the easiest form of government by sympathetic co-operation. Public policy does indeed involve assistance from *all* citizens; but the amount of enthusiasm, service, or acquiescence which each gives is different. No modern government is possible without some mobilized support on the part of the common man, which is more than mere acquiescence; and the rule of the majority is merely one method of securing adequate support. The minorities who acquiesce do indeed contribute their acquiescence to the co-operation provided by the majority; but under that system it is always possible to change the group which is willing to work together. Clearly, sometimes, the actual group in control may be numerically fewer than those who do not belong to that group; but even in such a case the co-operative power of the largest minority is not undemocratic, for government depends not on how many will *not* act together, but on how many will. A comparatively small group may be the best group to have control, if the rest of the community are not agreed to do anything but oppose them. The group in control has the moral right to co-operate among themselves for the common good, if it is the largest group of persons able to co-operate on *some* policy. It follows that "proportional representation", however useful for a debating society, is useless as a means of establishing an instrument of government; for government is the actual carrying out of some policy in daily administrative acts and in legislation.[1] Thus, a numerical minority of individuals may rightly have more power than a numerical majority; for voting is to discover not the numbers only but the unity or grouping of members.[2]

It is implied, however, in this conception of a group control in government that the group in control does not use force or unjust oppression of criticism in order to prevent the formation of other groups. The democratic ideal implies that, although at any one moment one policy is the basis of co-operation, nevertheless another policy may come to be practicable as another basis. The acquiescence of those not in agreement with the policy dominant at any time implies only allowing the "other fellow" to see what he can do; but clearly what he can do may prove to be unsatisfactory, or the common man may desire to see other policies tried. The essence of democracy, therefore, is not to be found in the fact that a numerically greater number of any community control the situation, but

[1] In addition, there are objections to proportional representation on democratic grounds, because in most schemes the constituencies would be too large, and therefore the severance of the representative from his constituents too great, and secondly, "first choices" and "second choices" are counted by the mere chance of the order of the voting papers.

[2] It is not a valid argument against Fascism or Communism that there are more non-Fascists or non-Communists in any community than there are Fascists or Communists, if the non-Fascists or non-Communists are not willing to work together otherwise than merely to oppose.

in the fact that there is an equal play of many minorities, one of which may be the only large group of men willing to act together for one policy. A flock of sheep or a crowd of homogeneous minds is not a democracy because it lacks internal structure. The democratic ideal, on the other hand, implies a society in which the natural psychological variations in the group-structure of consciousness have free play.

The common man, then, in so far as he is competent, is called into consultation through his choice of persons specially able to speak for the common good. But what is the consultation about? What are Councils and Parliaments for? It is only too easy to reply that they are for the making of laws or regulations and to avoid discussing the present character of such products of consultation.[1] We are obsessed with origins. Once upon a time laws were regarded simply as statements of established custom by a specially inspired king. Laws, in fact, were not conceived to be made, but only to be acknowledged and expressed; and when a restatement of an old custom was seen to be inadequate, the only method of meeting the new needs was to use such actual governmental powers as existed in order to set up a new system. But governmental power was autocratic, and laws were therefore regarded as the will of a sovereign. The sovereign could be controlled by the unwillingness of his subjects to pay what he required, and thus in practice the subject had power over the law; but law-making was conceived to be the exercise of an authority *over others*. The acquiescence of these others was called "the will of the people"; and the inevitability of tyranny was called "self-government". This theory and the practice based on it went on swimmingly until the middle of the nineteenth century.

Within the past fifty years, however, as indicated above, the functions of government have been transformed. The old

[1] Local Authorities, as they are called in Great Britain, are obviously only in part legislatures. As administrations they have been dealt with in the preceding chapter.

functions still survive for war and the punishment of crime; but they are now embedded in a mass of new functions quite unknown to Hobbes and Rousseau and Hegel and Spencer. Political science has advanced faster in blue-books than in treatises, because in treatises commentary on obsolete authorities has obscured the observation of contemporary facts. When, therefore, the new functions were undertaken in the art of government, the decisions as to policy, the laying down of the rule to be followed, changed in character. Modern legislation includes chiefly the establishment of new administrative machinery and the regulation of the normal action of citizens in view of new public needs. The laws establish a National Health Commission, an Authority for education, a system of unemployment insurance; they also indicate that citizens must lick stamps, must send their children to school, must avoid spitting in public places. To conceive all this as a command of a superior or the exercise of sovereign authority is atavistic. To imply that the disobeying of such laws is "crime" in the old sense, is merely to use an obsolete word for a new situation. But men do not move fast in their thoughts; and they are slower still in changing their language. The learned are the slowest of all, because they know the old jargon best; whereas the common man tends naturally to bad language, which is contemporary and expressive.

Therefore, the new situation was explained by the learned as the exercise of the sovereign authority of the Legislature. Parliaments tried to wear the robes of mediæval sovereigns; and, worse still, the miserable electors, driven from pillar to post by self-chosen representatives, were told that they were "the sovereign people". This faith is still untroubled in America. But clearly there is no sovereign in the old sense. Laws are not commands. They are agreements between equals as to (1) what acts each shall perform or (2) what acts shall be performed by their servants for the whole community.

As an example of the new situation, the work of the British

Parliament indicates the character of legislation. Sir Courtenay Ilbert, lately Clerk to the House of Commons, has described the new system.[1] "When authors of books on jurisprudence", he says, "write about law, when professional lawyers talk about law", they are thinking of contracts, torts, property law, and the law of family relations, or about the law of crimes in the Penal Code. All this is "lawyers' law". But nowadays Parliament hardly touches law in that sense. The "substantial business of Parliament as a legislature" is to keep the machinery of the State in working order. Since 1832, that is, when the modern State arose, most laws have been administrative regulations; and it is in this period that "Englishmen first began to realize the potentialities of the modern State". There has been "a complete remodelling, due to the shift of the centre of gravity since 1832", or, as expressed above, under the influence of the democratic ideal. The result is "an administrative machine of great complexity", in which the common man forms an integral part.

The transformation of the character of law is still in progress. The new legislation is beginning to affect the old. The treatment of criminals is being changed and "punishment" is becoming obsolete. Sanctions, if that obsolete word must still be used, are no longer the force of a superior, but the debt of honour to be paid for violation of an agreement. A moral change is occurring which is too fundamental for discussion here; but it can be seen operative in the practice by which legislative assemblies now regulate the growth of social life.

New laws, then, are rearrangements to meet new social needs;[2] and the common man in consultation is useful, first, because he can express such needs through his representatives, and, secondly, because the reorganization involved usually requires some co-operation from him. He assists, therefore, in making the law partly at least because he has to carry it out;

[1] *Legislative Methods and Forms*, pp. 209, 213, etc.

[2] See Roscoe Pound, *The Philosophy of Law.*

and it is found in practice more likely that co-operation in a new order will occur if those who have to co-operate have some feeling that their co-operation is dependent upon their own willingness. Circumstances change. The habits of a village will not fit a city area; for example, drainage must be introduced when men live in close contact. Adjustment of daily practice must be made; the rule of custom must be modified; and since it is a rule for common men, the more of them brought into consultation somehow in the process of modification, the easier the change, the smoother the transition. Again, if they are brought in, the new rule is more likely to be suitable to such abilities as its operation may require. That is why the franchise is extended to all whose conscious co-operation in the new daily acts is requisite; and that is why it is quite impossible to leave out women.

In modern circumstances, it is not possible for one man or a small group of men to change habits without regard to what their neighbours are doing. But natural forces as well as the incidental results of an increased birth-rate or crowding into towns make some changes of habit necessary. A daily modification of old habits occurs; and legislation is a method of making "mutations" that are more drastic than small accretions in social evolution. But these "mutations" are more speedily and smoothly made when they are made in view of a new series of daily acts. A legislature, therefore, should always be closely related to the administration. The art of government remains an art of acting every day, not of facing crises; and the consultation of common men, therefore, has in view not merely a possible jump over a difficulty but a journey on the other side. The need for the common man in consultation arises out of the nature of the journey to be made; for all law is an experiment. No one knows beforehand how an agreement to co-operate on certain lines will affect the whole situation, and therefore in modern legislation much detail may be left to the administration to be decided, as experience shows the way. At every step, as indicated above, the common man should be consulted, if democracy is to prevail—not because of any sentimental worship of the common man but because, as State services touch him more intimately, his daily acts must be adjusted in view of such services.

Consultation remains subordinate to action. The Council or Parliament, in so far as it is not an executive but a legislature, is subordinate in the art of government to the Administration, in the sense explained above. And this subordination is preserved in the forms of the British tradition. The Crown calls the Parliament to consult only because there is special need for occasional consultation. The Lords of Parliament, selected by the mediæval Civil Service,[1] are summoned by a writ which even to-day emphasizes "the weightiness of the affairs and imminent perils" on which they are to "give counsel". The writ to Sheriffs and Mayors who direct the election of the representatives of the Commons, asks only for their names; and the Members are summoned to hear the King's speech. It is true that when the speech is over the Houses change the subject and do business of their own, discussing a formal Bill on Vestries, for example, in order to show that even the Crown cannot define the limits of their competence. But as a Legislature they have been called together by the Crown; they do not come together of their own motion.[2]

Again, the Crown is not the King. When the King opens Parliament, he is preceded to the Parliament House by a carriage in which comes the Crown itself, which is given a special salute and honours; and when the King has departed, the Crown itself again goes in a special carriage with its escort, not to the

[1] See Pollard's *History of Parliament*, where it is shown that the Lords of Parliament are an accidental selection from the mediæval barons, bishops, and other notables. The Civil Service made the first Parliament in Great Britain.

[2] In certain Dominions the position of the Crown in the calling of Parliament does not seem to be understood; for the theory of Parliamentary sovereignty has confused the situation. The Crown in Parliament is not subordinate to Parliament.

King's dwelling but to the Palace of the Court of St. James. The King, wearing the Crown, reads the Speech to those who have been called into consultation, and that mysterious entity the Crown thus continues to govern. This Crown is probably the Commonwealth itself acting every day as one whole; but in any case in the British tradition the machine of government as a whole subordinates the function of deciding policy at crises, which is legislation, to daily acts, which is administration.

Representative assemblies remain, in this theory, supreme in the direction of policy, in the choice of the journey to be undertaken, and in the continual criticism of those who have to organize the journey. If that is sovereignty in Parliament, then sovereignty survives, and the Executive in a democracy is "responsible" to the common man through his elected representatives. But a moral responsibility rests upon the common man in his decision as to the course to be followed; and the agent or official has a moral responsibility not only to follow the course but also to see, from his point of vantage, that the course is right. The functions to be performed in political democracy are more numerous and various than they are in any other form of government. The art of government under the influence of the democratic ideal has yet to be learnt; but it is a less primitive art than command and obedience, and it would be foolish indeed to blame the democratic ideal for defects in a machinery of government which it has inherited from the confusions of the past.

The arguments therefore against the disuse or abolition of representative bodies are as follows: First, the bringing into play for use in government of the abilities of common men cannot be so well achieved without some form of consultation in which they are represented. The fact that common men are not well represented is no proof that they should not be. And unless they hear what is about to be done, they lack interest in the system. They will not lift a finger to help a government of which they know nothing, if it is in danger. Secondly, the educational value of electoral issues is lost without some effort at representation of common men; and therefore, as each year passes without consultation of common men, the established system becomes more unintelligible. But if men do not understand either what they are doing or what is being done, they are unlikely to do what is best, even for a tyranny. Thirdly, without representative bodies, there is no "opposition". Criticism driven underground, is not sufficiently close to the facts and, being less well-informed, becomes more drastic. All political wisdom in a dictatorhip is assumed to be in the possession of the same small group over a series of years. But long periods of office separate the holder of office from the solid earth of common life. An irremovable dictator tends upwards into the clouds, from which he may indeed thunder, but cannot speak in an intelligible voice. The lack of representative bodies therefore increases the gap between governors and governed, which makes the modern functions of government difficult or impossible to perform. Modern government needs the consultation, because it needs the daily co-operation, of the common man.

No one denies that existing representative assemblies are defective; but even if an automobile does not work well, it is foolish to go back into a farm cart, however romantic. The defects of the House of Commons are not proofs of the excellences of the House of Lords. Ability is not always inherited, and the test of the sort of ability required for modern legislation is candidature at an election, not being a pro-consul or a judge or a bishop. Assemblies for debate or criticism by specialists or by the aged and experienced may be useful for publicity and the general education of citizens, but not for decisions. But survivals need not be abolished; there are other and more skilful methods of dealing with them. In any case the only form of legislature which can be reconciled with the democratic ideal is a representative assembly, in the sense explained above, because legislation is an agreed decision as to acts to be done by common men or in their name.

The further progress towards political vitality in any community which accepts the democratic ideal undoubtedly depends upon the common man. The common man's natural tendency to associate in a common task with his fellows can be used much more fully; and it is possible for the simplest of men to understand the claims and interest of others. He expects, very justly, that his own ability to enjoy and to act shall have a place; but most men recognize that that place is made by agreement with those with whom they are in contact, and obviously another man will make place for you more willingly, if you make place for him. The adjustment of forces in a new situation is one of the purposes for which the common man chooses representatives. Therefore, democracy is not the control of the majority over a minority, but a balancing of minorities; and skill in political life is not merely voting on the right side but acting together with one's fellows in a common task. It requires no small skill to act with those whose opinions are opposed to one's own; but the common man has that skill more abundantly than most of his guides.

Clearly, common men see that each derives advantage from a "give and take": and the pursuit of a common interest may be induced by the belief that the share for each separate interest will be great. But that phraseology tends to be misleading. The doctrine of selfishness is not made less diabolical, if the selfishness is called "enlightened". The assumption implied is denied to be valid in the earlier portion of this book—namely, that men are fundamentally segregate units. The truth is that a common interest is not merely an addition of a sum of private interests, for my interest and yours in some cases may be identical. The health of one's neighbour's child is a necessary means to the health of one's own child, and is therefore one's own interest. The establishment of a system of roads or a rule of the road convenient for others is a convenience for one's self. These are goods of each in which all share.

But the tendency to fellowship among common men is the

psychological basis for a still deeper understanding of the common good. The common man's ability is underestimated if it is imagined that he is only scrambling for a part of the pile. It is too low an appeal to make rhetoric out of grievances and claims. Clearly there is much meanness. Loose thinking, to the effect that each can grab more without giving, may be found among those who advocate reforms; but narrow thinking among the opponents of reform is commoner. It would indeed be foolishly romantic to idealize the common man; but on the other hand, it is a very narrow realism which sees in him only what is evil and ugly, for the common man is not merely an appetite for more. How can that be proved? Treat men as noble and they are ennobled. Ask men to sacrifice themselves and they will do it—alas! only too readily, as the bloody waste of war has shown. Such is the proof that a common good can be conceived by common men without reference to their share in it. Therefore representatives who speak only of the private grievances or private gains of their constituents obstruct the advance of democracy and underestimate the abilities of the common man. The problem of politics is not merely a reconciliation of opposing powers or interests but an extension in practice, that is to say, in daily acts and periodical decisions, of the understanding of the common good by the common man.

This common good is not mine and yours but the good of a larger whole, whose character can be understood best by supposing that it affects not you and me but the relation between us. Men are related in many ways. They work together in business or manufacture. They play together; they live together in houses. It is a common good when the relations between men are such as to give their abilities free play. It is a common good when the structure of government is such that men do not feel it a burden. In this sense then, quite apart from the benefits you and I may receive, the State is a common good. But the "tone" of the relations between men in one community differs from the "tone" in other communities. Democracy implies a certain tone or atmosphere in the way men treat other men politically, so that each allows the others liberty to act and to speak and all assist in devising and maintaining the rule by which daily habits are formed. There may be no such community yet in existence; for laws are still felt to be limitations of liberty and liberty is still thought to be my right, not another's. But the changes that have recently occurred, both in representation and in legislation, seem to indicate that we are at the beginning of a release of new abilities among common men: and the common man already has his eyes upon horizons more distant than private grievances and private gains.

CHAPTER V

WAR AND DEMOCRACY

POLITICAL democracy is a system for the transformation of authority into service as the binding force of social life. It displaces the older virtue of obedience by the newer virtue, co-operation. In government it involves the gradual change from acquiescence of the majority into contribution by all to a common service. The State becomes a source of direct benefit to all citizens and not, as it was and still is outside the democratic tradition, a means of culture for the few through the subservience of the rest of the community. But as benefits are more equally distributed, obligations have to be more generally undertaken; for modern government cannot increase health, education, or the opportunities for wealth unless all citizens assist in the common task. And obligations have been undertaken successfully by common men who have been during the past fifty years under the influence of the democratic ideal. The modern State is established.

A great number of States of this kind already exist. They differ in details of the machinery of government. But in all of them the common man contributes some thought and some emotional sympathy with his fellows. In the Scandinavian countries, in Great Britain, the British Dominions, Holland, the United States, and for the past ten years in Germany, all adult men and women have a share in the common responsibility. Thus there are common men in this and that land who pursue their common ends through distinct governments. The progress of the democratic tradition has led each group to the organization of modern government as far as a frontier; and there the system of organization of each group comes to an end. The modern State is still undeveloped in its relation with other States. The citizen of each State is divided from the citizen of other States.

Between each group and the other are "defences"—navies and bombing aircraft, armies and fortifications. Within each State force has diminished—punishment of crime is less cruel, the police are directors of traffic rather than catchers of criminals, the confidence of common men, each in the other, is extended; but at the frontier force has increased, suspicion is more continuous and new thought, energy, and expense are daily devoted to devising new instruments of destruction and new plans of attack. War and the preparation for war lie across the path that democracy has to follow.

The relation between States is so primitive that in this matter the history of the future depends not on the use of the instruments, but on the discarding of old instruments and the invention of new. It may be possible to beat swords into ploughshares; but probably the best plan would be to leave the sword to rust and make the ploughshare out of new steel. In any case, it is quite impossible to plough with a sword. But the State, in its external relations, is still more like a sword than a plough. Its citizens, with regard to the citizens of any other State, are still too often in the posture of gladiators; and policy is still based very largely upon the assumption that across a frontier is an armed camp and not a market. And all the traditional assumptions which serve as "covers" or as rationalizations of this situation, whatever their historical explanation or justification, are now not only obsolete but positively obstructive to civilized life.

The situation survives largely because it is not envisaged in detail. The burden of armaments is not noticed because it has been borne for so long; but out of every shilling paid in taxation in Great Britain, ten years after "the war to end war" about eightpence goes to pay for war and only about fourpence for all the services of peace under the central government. Most of the payment for war is the debt for past wars, still weighing down new generations, but about threepence in the shilling is for "defence" in future wars. And all nations are thus burdened. Recently, indeed, the Paris Pact for the Renunciation of War "as an instrument of national policy", should have decreased the need for defence, but so far no difference has been made in preparations for a new war. Again, gas-warfare and skill in bombing from aeroplanes are being made more efficient every day. Good brains and youthful energy are being spent in perfecting the ability to kill men and to destroy the means of civilized life; and this is understood to be the service of the State! The State to which one belongs is thus conceived, not as an organization for public health or education or roads, but as an armed band; and the State to which one does not belong is conceived only as an obstacle to the service of one's own State.

With the preparation for war goes the planning of new wars, in case they should occur. Alliances breed military conventions. Organizing ability is wasted in devising strategic tricks against this or that possible enemy; and "secret services" work for each State to corrupt the allegiance of citizens of the other States and to worm out secrets that ought not to exist. The atmosphere of intercourse between governments is poisoned by suspicion of what each is preparing to do in case war should occur. Commerce is impeded on the ground that no State can afford to risk dependence upon foreigners for food or munitions of war, in case war should occur. And all this is done by the State which, as was shown above, during the past fifty years in civilized communities has become a centre of public services. So long as government was only policing it was not ridiculous to suppose that force was its chief means of action; but now that government is a system of public health and education, the preparation for war goes against its very nature. Every step in such preparation hinders any step in the new development of the art of government, and every State which is a public service, by preparing for war, hinders every other State from being a public service.

It is quite impossible in such an atmosphere for the development to continue which has been traced in the preceding chapters. If each State is a system of co-operaton between common men for health, education, organized production, and consumption, not to speak of a quiet life, then co-operation should not stop at frontiers. The health of the citizens of one State may be destroyed by epidemics spreading from foreigners. Bacteria do not respect frontiers. Knowledge cannot expand within frontiers; for the supply of genius in any community is small and use may be found for foreign genius. To obstruct commerce, lest it may be obstructed in the future, is to introduce beforehand the barbarism against which preparation is to be made. And even domestic peace and quiet is easier to obtain if men on the other side of one's frontier are peaceful. Therefore, whatever hinders co-operation between the citizens of different States prevents the development of the services of the modern State even for its own citizens.

Secondly, the expenditure of money, and still more of brains and energy, in the preparation for war decreases the amount available for improving the conditions of normal life. The annual cost of a large navy would more than supply the funds necessary to lengthen the lives of common men by three years: that is to say, if we could abolish armaments, existing men and women could have longer lives, less weakened by illness and more enjoyable. The cost of war should thus be reckoned in terms of the abilities of common men. And in every nation in which conscription is established there is a waste of months or years which might, if there were no danger of war, be put into productive industry, the increase of knowledge and skill in the arts of peace and more subtle enjoyments. Indeed, the long years of preparation for wars that do not occur are almost as wasteful as war itself.

Thirdly, democracy, as explained above, implies diverse contributions from different men and groups of men, who disagree in their views of public policy and suggest different lines of action; and this implies confidence in those who differ from one's own views and free criticism of any policy that happens for the moment to be followed. But modern war involves regimentation of a whole community. The new French Law of mobilization for war includes all women as well as men among the forces of the State. The old distinction between combatants and non-combatants is obsolete, as is the distinction between contraband and free goods. In war all must obey a single will which may be mistaken and yet must not be criticized. Secrecy as to what is intended is useful against an enemy, and deceiving enemies affects citizens as well as enemies. The ability to doubt what is official, essential in democracy, is diminished; and passions are inflamed which are difficult to control. But if that is the state of a population at war, the preparation for war forms the basis for that regimentation by propaganda and autocratic decisions. The more docile and ignorant the population, the more easily will men be frightened by bugbears and made to hate those whose languages or habits are unfamiliar, the more possible it is to show that all the right is on the one side and all the wrong on the other. But the preparation for war in drilling youths to kill foreigners and in paying for armaments is maintained by spreading or reviving fear or suspicion and inducing the uncritical acceptance of traditional military authorities. The more simple-minded any man is, the more firmly he believes that the bad habits of his grandfathers are inevitable. Again, the less criticism is allowed, the more easily it will be believed that the interests of one's own country can be maintained by force of arms and not by argument in a judicial procedure. Thus the social "tone", the abilities needed in a democracy, and the habits of mind essential for democratic government are obstructed, if not actually in some persons destroyed, by the preparations for war. The progress of democracy requires, therefore, the elimination of the danger of war.[1]

[1] It is to be hoped that no one now living is quite so foolish as Hegel in supposing that war ennobles men. The virtues incidental to war can be

It is perhaps believed that war is still probable; and that therefore there is an unfortunate necessity to prepare for it. But this argument is not valid. In the first place there are degrees of probability, and the preparation for war increases the probability of its occurring. Each nation's defence force, as it becomes more efficient, becomes more dangerous to its neighbours: and therefore induces an increase in the efficiency of other defence forces. But the more elaborate the preparation, the more subtle the strategy and the more urgent the search for allies, until the strain is suddenly broken by an accident. And yet those who prepare armaments and strategies really believe that their activities add to security, in spite of the fact that they have to increase public nervousness in order to induce the public to pay for more armaments. The strongest argument, however, against the preparation for war is not that it causes war, but that a deliberate policy of peace could destroy the need for it, and that war itself could be abolished by agreed action between any group of powerful nations. The method is simply that already tried in the Greek-Bulgarian dispute of 1926, or the Bolivia-Paraguay dispute of 1928: that is to say, the stopping of all armed conflict by international pressure. This is the procedure. Whenever there is actual fighting or the threat of immediate fighting *both parties* must be stopped. No inquiry need be made as to which is guilty of "aggression", and which is acting only in self-defence. That problem is irrelevant for the moment, since whoever is in the wrong, force is not the way to correct an error. Even the right of self-defence is transitional, for it is in abeyance as soon as there is public force on the scene. The first step is the prevention of resort to armed conflict by all the means in the hands of

cultivated under any disease. But no one believes it morally right to increase tuberculosis in order to give opportunities for endurance and pity. Again, the supposed instinct of pugnacity may be expressed by hitting one's neighbour and fellow-citizen, but it is not developed by sitting in frozen mud waiting for high explosives or gas from an enemy who is never seen. The romantic sentimentalism which surrounds the word "war" still obscures the facts in spite of some modern literature.

civilized Governments. The decision as to the grievances of the parties concerned in any conflict of interests may be given later by arbitration or conciliation or never given at all. But whether given or not, whether there is some other way of redressing grievances or not, war is ruled out. This is like the action of a policeman who simply stops a fight in the street, whether or not he arrests the combatants or brings them to court. But nations are not individuals; and one of the reasons for believing that force could be ruled out is that in every nation there is a group which would prefer in any given case not to use force. That group must be given support from outside.

This method of eliminating the danger of war rests upon (1) the acceptance of Article II of the Kellogg or Paris Pact, which forbids all attempts to settle disputes by other than peaceful means, and upon (2) the recognition of the duty of civilized nations to use their influence for the stopping of all war. No international force is needed for punishing aggressors or mutual "security". No nation or Government is called upon to take sides in a dispute or to "defend" any other nation, unless one party in a conflict actually stops and the other does not. The high seas, in such a policy, would be kept open for shipping and no fighting or stoppage of traders be allowed, even if a war arose between any two nations. Blockade would be regarded as piracy. Economic pressure, exclusion of foreign goods, alliances to "squeeze" rivals might occur, but not resort to arms: nor would such pressure or "squeezing", however reprehensible, be held to justify armed action by the aggrieved party.

With such a situation established, even experimentally, the preparation for war could be very greatly reduced, if not abandoned; and every step towards decreasing the preparation for war would make war itself less likely. The obstacles, however, to such a policy are not reasoned alternative policies, but atavisms and customary attitudes, which are still dominant among common men, of which the chief are (1) the conception of sovereignty and (2) the passion of nationalism.

The conception of sovereignty survives in the technical language of diplomacy and in some textbooks. In practice it is the atavism which limits co-operation between States and prevents Governments from submitting to judicial settlement of disputes. But in modern times even what is assumed when a State is treated as sovereign is very different from what it was in the Renaissance—the ancient time in which sovereignty was first conceived; for no one now thinks of sovereignty as an appeal against the claims of Pope or Emperor. The utility of having one authority supreme in law and administration over all inhabitants in a given territory—internal or domestic sovereignty, induced the jurists to suppose that externally or in inter-State relations there can be a similar supremacy or absolutism. There is no denying the validity of the practice and theory of *autonomy*. No State is or should be, subject to another; and any form of subjection is a diminution of Statehood or of the supremacy within the given territory of the particular form of law and administration there current. This does not mean that every small group should be autonomous. There is no practical or theoretical advantage in having an immense number of small States; and therefore it may be best for civilized life that the system of government in some areas should be in only a limited sense autonomous or should have its "foreign" relations organized under another system of government, which thus would be, in the old sense of the word, suzerain or sovereign. But the degree of autonomy which each political group should have is to be discovered in the art of government by "trial and error". The test is the amount of vitality in civilized life which such autonomy can produce. A very small group cannot live fully in the exercise of so difficult an art as that of modern government. And even a very large group which consists of unintelligent or primitive minds may not fare best with autonomy in every aspect of its public affairs.

But in the case of those areas or group of persons which are fully autonomous, their present relation to other areas or groups of the same kind cannot possibly be understood under the term sovereign, since supremacy has no meaning in reference to such a relation. However independent a chair and a table may be, it is ridiculous to try to discover in what way each is "supreme" in their relations. The result of such attempts is to suggest that there is no relation at all between States which do, in any case, exist on the same Earth. The reason for the use of the conception of sovereignty to include independence of external authority, as well as supremacy within a territory, in the Renaissance, was that shadowy claims were then made by the Papacy and the Holy Roman Empire. Obviously, the new national States and even the local chieftains of Germany could not maintain their authority, if appeals against them might be made to Pope or Emperor or other Suzerain. Sovereignty in external affairs therefore meant independence: but independence was conceived in negative terms, as isolation from control by a superior. And there was no reference in the conception or practice of sovereignty to connections between States. This implied denial of the existence of a State-system was always false, as Grotius saw; but it is ludicrous now. Independence cannot possibly mean absence of all relations. Autonomy, which is a better word than independence because it is not negative, should imply the positive contribution of each State to the maintenance, not only of its own "domestic jurisdiction", but also of the State-system, that is, of other States in relation to it. Thus autonomy of each unit in the State-system implies not independence but interdependence.

Governments, in so far as they promote order and liberty for their own people, cannot possibly aim at destroying order and liberty outside their jurisdiction without endangering their own existence; for just as disease spreads, and therefore England could not be healthy if England promoted disease in France, so disorder spreads. But war is the effort to spread disorder abroad, to undermine the confidence of foreign peoples in their own Governments, to make life unendurable under the foreign system: and the preparation for war is a continual planning of precisely this contamination of the system outside one's own frontiers. It is as absurd as planning to spread disease outside in order that the people outside may be so weak that they could not spread disease among us. The attitude of mind on which the preparation for war depends is obsolete; for it belongs to the time when it was still possible to imagine one's State to be a world apart, without being obviously a lunatic. In so far, therefore, as any Government still continues to prepare for war, even a war of self-defence, that Government is an atavism. But all Governments now prepare for war.

Sovereignty, however, is a conception of specialists. It may be implied in the attitude adopted by the common man in any State towards any foreign Government; but the common man is not aware of that implication. If, therefore, the obstacle to democratic progress which is to be found in the diplomatic and warlike practices based on sovereignty, is to be overcome, the common man must be enlightened. He must face the fact that he inherits his attitude towards other Governments from primitive times, and that an inherited attitude is obsolete when the circumstances which gave rise to it have ceased to exist.

The fundamental issue is the attitude of citizens in each State. The majority in all States and in most political groups within States are primitive in this matter at least—they do not think or feel beyond frontiers. They are like young children who do not think beyond the walls of their home: and there are, in every country, nursery "leaders" and youthful "soldiers" who, in praise of that excellent home, decry a more extensive geography. The obsolete conception of sovereignty in external affairs receives support from these ineptitudes; and the particular form of political simple-mindedness and nursery patriotism which is our present danger is called nationalism. This is an emotional belief held by a group of men to the effect that its blood or language or moral tradition or "country" is the source of all that is valuable or magnificent in the group life. The resulting passion is made the basis for a political scheme to establish a particular form of government in and for that group. Common men do actually feel this passion and maintain the beliefs of nationalism; and, indeed, it is much more pernicious in quasi-democratic societies than in circles which are aristocratically cynical. Modern nationalism is a disease of democracy in its nursery.

Upon this depends the institution called war. Obviously, this modern nationalism is not the origin of war, which was common long ago. Nor is nationalism the cause of war; for different wars have different causes and there is no one cause for wars as a class, just as there is no one cause for fits of anger or for standing on one's head. But the tendencies, impulses, complexes, habits, and instincts, which find an outlet in the preparations for and the waging of war, are in our time most actively organized in that peculiar attitude called nationalism. War cannot, therefore, become obsolete, and the preparation for it cannot cease, until the present form of nationalism disappears. Even then clearly some new superstition may arise. It is not impossible that great numbers may come to believe that the habits of red-haired men are an excuse for war. The gullibility of men is not to be underestimated. But—one obstacle at a time! It will be something accomplished in the obsolescence of war if the present form of nationalism dies down.

To overcome these obstacles to peace the abilities of the common man in imagination and intelligence must be increased. Nursery nationalism arises out of limited perception of actual facts. The idea that what is best in everyday life is local in origin may have been correct in the Middle Ages; but in every industrial country to-day most of the population use food and material for clothing which comes from afar. Any meal and any suit or dress provides a lesson in international intercourse. Indeed, the body of any man in a modern city area, in so far as it is built up out of Argentine meat, Indian tea, Brazilian coffee, and warmed by Australian wool and United States cotton—is an international object. The eyes that read this are physically international; but the mind in most men remains perversely national. Nursery nationalism is an inability to see facts.

Again, the security from and cure of disease and the methods of communication and travel are results of recent export and import of ideas. Civilized life is thoroughly international. The ideas of our countrymen cannot be disentangled from those of foreigners in science, art, commerce, or finance. But the actual situation is not visible to the common man largely because of the teaching of history from which he has suffered.

History is no longer a mere list of battles and kings, but it is still too much concerned with rivalries and too little concerned with the growth of co-operation between nations. Most men still know only the great men of their own country, and the foreign names remembered are those of warriors, not those of teachers. The contact with foreign nations is still regarded as having been exceptional in the past, even if such contacts are not described as conflicts, as they are in some modern school-books. In conflicts the histories put the emphasis upon those only in which our own nation can be presented as victorious. Wars are said to have ended in situations vaguely described as defeats or victories; but famine, disease, disorder, and the sufferings of common men, which are the inevitable results of all wars, whether "successful" or not, are not mentioned. Above all, the futility of all wars appears not to be perceived even by historians; for they never ask whether what was sought by war could not have been achieved otherwise. Art and science, commerce, and the comfort of common men, which have progressed by the continuous and increasing amicable contact between nations are mentioned in parentheses or not at all. It is not strange, then, that the common man cannot see what is under his nose and is living in a false mythology of national rivalries; but from the black magic of the traditional history he can be delivered only by the white magic of a new history which presents those facts most relevant to the interests and purposes of modern life.

A new teaching of history would give rise to a more enlightened patriotism. The children of each nation would learn what their own country had done for other countries in discovery, invention, art, the cure of disease, or skill in government. They would be proud of their country not for what it has got but for what it has given. And they would learn to regard other nations as groups of common men, like themselves, pursuing the same ends of peace and happier life, and useful to them in that pursuit. They would reckon as "France" the work of Pasteur and Corot: as "Germany" the work of Koch and Einstein: as "England" the work of Lister and Constable —to mention only modern names. And perhaps they would understand that we are at the beginning and not at the end of the history of civilization. Such an understanding releases abilities hitherto unused. Fear and suspicion of what is foreign or unusual are cured; and men are made ready to take part in a task which their forefathers began but could not accomplish because of the superstition, with which a false history surrounded them. The release of such abilities is a task for parents and teachers.

The overcoming of the other obstacle to co-operation between peoples, the habit arising out of the conception of sovereignty, is a problem of politics. That, too, depends ultimately upon education: but it can be immediately faced by deliberate policy. The policy of peace is the increase of co-operation for common advantage between Governments. This eliminates the habits based upon sovereignty, without even denying the truth of the ideas on which they rest. Modern government aims at the increase of the vitality of citizens by the better provision of the conditions of health, the organization of education, the improvement and extension of industry and trade. All these methods of civilizing life can best be used if there is co-operation between the administrative departments of the Governments concerned. It follows that a natural and inevitable development of modern government is a system of co-operation between Governments for certain definite purposes; because, whatever rivalries remain, at least in that system the habit of co-operation would be learnt.

There is already such a system: it is the League of Nations. Not all States form part of that system, which is regrettable, but mainly from the point of view of citizens in States which are *not* members; for if there is any advantage in the League, such citizens do not have their full share. It is possible that it would be better for those now members of the League if other States also joined it: but whether it would be better would depend upon (1) the ability or willingness to co-operate in the system on the part of new-comers and upon (2) whether the system in the State newly entering was suitable for interlocking with the system of those already members. Thus the League *might* be improved by the entry of Russia and the United States, if the Governments of these countries "played the game" and did not obstruct the work of the system, and secondly, if the system for ratifying treaties and undertaking obligations, for example in social legislation, "ran in gear" with the administrative systems at present utilizing the League. On the other hand, perhaps some present members of the League are not "playing the game"; and if so, the League system would operate more successfully if they would resign. Nothing is to be gained by the adherence of unbelievers. Diplomatic politeness to established Governments should not go so far as to welcome a swashbuckler to the council chamber or a bankrupt to a directors' meeting.

But the membership of the League and the work already done by the use of the League system of co-operation are well known. Here the argument looks forward. What must be done in the near future to eliminate the dangerous tendencies in international affairs and to release the ability of the common man for the enjoyment of peace? The League system must be used for the dissolving of current enmities, grievances, or fears. But that cannot be done by soothing speeches nor by preaching the gospel of contentment to those who suffer injustice; and it would be fantastic to imagine that enmities and grievances are all unjustifiable. There is injustice in the relation of peoples: and some injustice is consecrated by Treaties. The first task is to revise such Treaties, not only because of the people who suffer wrong, but because the maintenance of a Treaty against which there is a very strong feeling that it is unjust, weakens the effectiveness of all Treaties. Why is so much thought devoted to planning assistance for one State in case another State breaks its pledge? It is because Treaty obligations are felt to be weak. And Treaty obligations are, in fact, weak, chiefly because of the many Treaties which are the results of *force majeure*. While therefore the enforcement of the prohibition of war, referred to above, is made more effectual, the whole basis of inter-State relations must be transformed. But this cannot be done by rhetoric or the promulgation of virtuous resolutions. It must be undertaken in detail, with regard to distinct and specific issues, for the discussion of which personal ability in friendly negotiation is more valuable than the knowledge of experts. Indeed, the unofficial diplomacy of groups of common men may do more than the conventional procedure of the officials, who pull the strings which make "statesmen" move and appear to speak.

Short of established injustice, there are incidental oppressions which the League system should relieve or forestall. Domestic or internal oppressions can never be dealt with by an association of States; and if any attempt is made by the League or through the League to suppress internal rebellion against any Government or to enforce any particular system of government upon a people against their will, the League will become a "Holy Alliance"—it will dissolve and ought to dissolve. But within the competence of an inter-State system is the relation of a small State to a Great Power. The League system should provide means whereby a small State may not suffer pressure financially, commercially, or militarily from any Great Power; but if so, then it must also provide a means whereby the responsibilities of Governments in small States are brought home to them. Imperialism is frequently attacked: but disorder in small States and incompetence and selfishness of a group in control in such a State are also evils. The solutions of problems thus arising in the contact of States must be thought out in practical detail. Vague complaints, even at League meetings, and equally vague admonitions to complainants are quite inadequate. But in the League system there should be (1) provision for the open discussion of complaints by one Government against another, (2) provision for investigation of the relevant factors by international Commissions, and (3) enough "pressure", diplomatic or economic, to ensure respect for the findings of such Commissions.

The second great group of tasks to be undertaken under the League system is economic. Financial problems such as the supply of capital for stabilizing a situation or for developing new resources which are valuable internationally, possibly the exchanges, and the levelling up of deteriorating currencies —all these are problems in the modern world which need an inter-State system for solution. Commercial problems must quite consistently be treated as international. It is absurd to suppose that a tariff is a purely domestic matter, though we may be a long way from the possibility of making all regulation of inter-State commerce dependent upon international agreement.[1] Would the British Parliament, for example, consent to wait for international agreement before imposing a new tariff on motor-cars? Would the British people recognize in practice that if a tariff on lace and embroidery is established, it affects employment in Switzerland, and therefore ought to be discussed with the Swiss? Clearly we have not reached that stage of development; but in practice the League system can be used for adjusting the interests of different peoples with regard to tariffs and other such obstacles to trade.

The so-called "Labour" problems or problems of the conditions of employment and the organization of industry are also in many cases international. The very timid and tentative treatment of such problems in the International Labour Organization and—in regard to slavery and forced labour—by other organs of the League, will have to be more vigorous. If the League system is taken seriously, it is not simply for the avoidance of war, but for making such peace as exists better "worth while" for the majority of men. Peace is inexcusable if it is simply an opportunity for securing the exploitation of some by others. Peace should be the occasion for the increase of justice among men in all their relations. But in practice this would involve that the League system or, failing the presence of certain States in the League, some similar international system, should be used to deal with such problems as Migration. In theory, everyone can see that movements of population from State to State create international problems; but in practice—will Australia consider any other interest than her own in admitting immigrants? Or will the United States? It will probably take more than ten years to break down the "frontier" sentiment in new States; but we may

[1] The Hides, etc., Agreement of August 1928, secured under League auspices, "constitutes the first collective Convention in existence in the sphere of tariffs". By this means the abolition of all prohibitions on the export and import of hides, skins and bones, has been secured. The products are unimportant: the principle is new. See *League Document*, C. 379, 1928

hope that there will be at least an increase of consultation as regards migration between different States.

The present hesitation of Australia and the United States in admitting immigrants is not unreasonable. Experience has shown that wages can be under-cut by imported "labour" and that a standard of civilized life can be reduced to chaos, if not quite destroyed, by a flood of unassimilable immigrants. The emigration of Jews and Poles from the oppression and ignorance in which they were kept by the pre-war Russia, that of Slavs and Czechs from poverty or similar oppressions in the old Empire of Austria-Hungary, increased very greatly the public burdens of the people of the United States. Similarly, it is by no means an international duty for Australia or Canada to take any persons who cannot find employment in Great Britain. On the other hand, the policy of a dog in the manger, even from the lowest point of view, is unwise in new States with undeveloped resources. What can reasonably be expected in the near future is an increase of international agreements on migration between the States chiefly concerned.

Other "labour" matters of an international kind include the regulation of hours and of the lowest rates of wages; but to deal with such matters involves the acceptance of some standard of life in many different States. No one imagines that the Japanese worker must be given wages enough to enable him to discard rice and eat wheat; but again, the modern world requires the consideration of such problems on a scale much larger than that of the traditional economic policy of States.

The field for the increase in co-operation between governments is immense. Skill in co-operation or even in the consultation which must precede it, is still inadequate. Knowledge of the facts of international intercourse is still childish, even among the leaders of men. But the elimination of war, which is essential for the progress of the democratic ideal, requires both knowledge and skill. Peace is not easy. It is not a sentiment nor a sleep. It requires more intelligence, more imagination, and greater ability than war and the preparation for war. But never before in history has there been so much youthful ability in democratic nations devoted to the organizations of peace. Groups of men and women, much more able and active than General Staffs, are at work in many nations at the actual promotion of co-operation between peoples. They are not yet in control of the situation. But peace is not improbable; and the next ten years will provide the test of the ability to secure it.

The common man will have to face that test; and the problem for the common man with regard to international affairs is mainly a problem in imaginative sympathy. Can the common man feel that he has an interest in the health or wealth of those who live outside his frontiers? Must diverse languages and traditions always make it impossible for the citizens of one State to co-operate with those of another? The trouble is that service of the State in war by the common man is generally understood; and that service has reference to other States. But service of the State in peace, if it is conceived at all, has usually no reference whatever beyond frontiers. A new teaching of history, however, as indicated above, might cure such blindness; for then it would be seen that the maintenance of State service in any State is a service rendered to other men in other States, and that the duty of a citizen to his fellow-men includes a duty towards the citizens of other States. Citizenship is in part the maintenance of peace and co-operation across frontiers. That is to say, it is the duty of a citizen of Great Britain not only not to hinder, but positively to promote the liberty and vitality of the citizens of France, Germany, and other States. The process of education in such citizenship will take time; and it is doubtful if we have ten years to spare. Another great war is being prepared. The tendencies towards such a war became stronger between 1925 and 1928; and although more peaceful tendencies may reassert themselves, the risk is great. Before the understanding of civilized life is advanced enough, the drift towards another great war may become too strong to control; for it is quite impossible to prevent such a war, if the tendencies towards war have been allowed to increase during many years. Every war is inevitable the day before it breaks out. No war is inevitable five years before the crisis which may cause it. The time to make peace is now.

But the effectual willingness to co-operate with foreigners, or the half-conscious habit of working together for permanent peace, is limited to a few only in a large community. Different groups of men think and feel about different enjoyments or occupations; and in a large community such as a nation, some groups are moved by football matches, others by dog-racing, others by local gossip. One among the many groups in any State may be following with interest the intercourse of nations in commerce, politics, or culture. In normal times the dog-racing group has no "opinion" about international affairs; but if a crisis approaches or a dispute arises between their own nation and another, they become excited under the influence of orators or journalists, who know how to play upon simple minds. The situation then becomes dangerous, because minds familiar only with dog-racing or football simplify the issue and stir in their atavistic depths. Thus the group which has been for many years following the turns of international intercourse may be swept aside by all the groups which have paid no attention to it. The danger, therefore, of allowing a crisis to approach in international intercourse is that it gives an opportunity for the dog-racing or football mind to take control of public policy. The common man is not a fool, if he prefers dog-racing to diplomacy. But those common men who have other tastes than dog-racing, and who prefer peace to war, must learn so effectually to influence the current of affairs in normal times that no crisis will throw them aside. The policy of peace prevents disputes arising, whatever means may exist for deciding them peacefully if they have arisen. And the function of that small group which is actively interested in promoting co-operation between Governments and peoples is to work continuously to increase the number and strength of the strands which bind men across frontiers. This, however, does not imply turning away from one's own country. The common man travelling abroad or looking for benefits from abroad in art, science, or useful goods, if he is skilled, is expressing a new patriotism, in regarding his own country as worthy of admiration and service because of the service it has rendered and will render to other nations in the common enterprise of civilized life. No doubt this implies the development of new abilities among common men. An imaginative sympathy, not yet strong enough nor widely enough spread in any nation, must bring into play new interests and new energies. But there are signs that it is coming. The wireless and the cinema make distant peoples almost familiar. Commerce and travel, in spite of obstacles maintained or newly invented by reactionary groups, are increasing; and even politicians and journalists seem to be aware that the simpler beliefs in "foreign devils" are fading. Much intellectual progress is needed before peace is secure. But the common man is already much less gullible than his instructors suppose, and too many Nobodies know what war is like for the belief that it is inevitable to overcome their suspicion that it is generally the result of the incompetence of superior persons.

CHAPTER VI

THE COMMON MAN IN INDUSTRY

THE common man is, in the terms of the Census, an "occupied person", employed most of his waking life in producing goods or rendering services for payment. His relations to government are affected by his occupation mainly because his mental structure, his attitude, his habitual reactions, and his complexes are the results of what he is doing to "make a living". The abstract man, therefore, of the earlier democratic theory, who had "natural rights" and apparently nothing to do except to vote occasionally, is irrelevant for practical policy in social life. Men and women must be considered as coal-miners, railway workers, textile workers, agricultural labourers, or charwomen and cooks, before any conclusion can be made as to how or why they should vote or obey laws; for each of these classes of men and women has a distinct and characteristic outlook and behaviour; and each characteristic outlook and behaviour is a group-factor or single social force in the life of a community. There is a mental structure in every nation or large community corresponding to its occupational structure. Men and women in agricultural districts do not think of the same things, nor feel the same kinds of emotion as dwellers in city areas who work in crowds. The psychological abilities therefore available in common men must be analysed in reference to their occupations.

The issues now to be discussed are, in one sense of the word, economic; that is to say, they affect directly the production and consumption of goods and services exchanged. The problem is whether the common man in these issues can be anything more than an instrument of a superior will. Can there be industrial democracy? Can boots and bread be produced and used, if the common man is allowed "a say" in the direction of economic policy? The answers to such questions affect the political situation; for if industry can be carried on only under an authoritarian system, then it is unlikely that political democracy will survive. If men and women in their occupations, that is in most of their waking lives, are merely passive tools, they cannot suddenly become contributors to policy or co-operators in public affairs when government is in question. On the other hand, those who have been given "a say" in government are not likely to remain without power over industrial policy. Fascism and Communism involve in practice even in industry subservience of the manual workers to superior authorities, over whom they have no control. Democracy, on the other hand, should involve contributions of thought and decision from the common man employed in the rendering of economic services.

Industrial democracy, however, does not necessarily take the same forms as political democracy, that is to say, voting for representatives and legislative assemblies. The purpose in political organization is order and liberty; but the purpose in economic organization is the production of boots and bread. Whatever therefore democracy means in industry, it must be mainly a system for the more efficient rendering and using of industrial services. The characteristic of industrial democracy will be the use of all such abilities of men as may be available for the advantage of all men. But because a man thinks and feels when he digs coal or drives an engine, therefore under the influence of the democratic ideal the system of production must give a place for his thinking and feeling, as well as for his muscular power; and because each man needs food and leisure for vitality, the system must provide all men with adequate supplies of these. The democratic ideal does *not* imply that the coal-hewer shall be a manager, nor the manager a coal-hewer; although it does imply that the selection of managers or directors shall be by a test of competence, not by birth or chance. And in the relation of the coal-hewer to the manager, the democratic ideal does *not* imply that the manager shall be controlled by the coal-hewer; although it does imply that the coal-hewer shall not be merely an instrument for the advantage of others. The democratic ideal, therefore, applied to the industrial system, raises two questions: one is the position, status, or function of those employed in production; the other is the distribution and use made of the goods and services available. Because all but a few are both producers and consumers, it is impossible, in devising policy, to separate the two issues. For example, if men starve they cannot work; and if work is not done, all will starve. But for the purpose of the argument here, the art of use or enjoyment or consumption may be discussed separately and attention may be given first to production.

The actual production of goods and the services rendered in the available supply of bread and boots are the results of psychological abilities, organized and used in what is now called the industrial system. But so familiar has this system become that the mental structure of habit and belief on which it rests is hardly considered. Men and women, as factory-workers or as clerks, go regularly day by day to the same places in crowds, work at the same routine, receive fixed amounts of the power to command services, and come to treat as the nature of things a social situation which is hardly a century old. It indicates a wide range of psychological abilities to be able to do all this. The common man is so built as to be able to bear up the industrial system. And the effects of the system confirm and expand these abilities of men and women. What they think and feel about their fellow-men, what they think about the State, or the Church, or the school, or art or literature—in so far as they have energy to spare for thinking in other than economic terms—all this is affected by the mechanization of their lives in industry. Their thoughts and feelings may be no worse for being so affected. It is an unwarranted assumption to suppose that the mental effects of modern economic activities are bad; but the facts must be reviewed as a preliminary, without approval or condemnation.

First, the situation is new and fundamentally different from any that has hitherto occurred. If the history of civilization since 6000 B.C. be represented by a line eight inches long, the history of the industrial system will be represented by less than an eighth of an inch at the end: and the mere shortness of the time for this new experiment is less striking than the revolutionary change in daily habits which it has required—a work regulated by the clock, at large machines in the work-places of crowds, distant from their homes. Secondly, therefore, the situation requires a widespread capacity for regular work, perhaps during a whole lifetime. That is the price of safety from famine and disorder. But thirdly, the situation requires an extensive ability for intricate forms of co-operation between men. For the majority of common men, the mere sense that other men are working at their elbows creates a new feeling of fellowship and new forms of sociability; and for the few the system involves an ability to devise and to maintain relations between men who never meet one another and would not understand one another if they did meet. Co-operation between men, which is involved in modern manufacture and commerce, has never hitherto existed on such a large scale. At first the new system developed in the traditional mediæval atmosphere of authoritarian religion and politics; and at a time when slavery was legally possible, if not actually practised in Europe, the new mechanisms attracted more attention from thinkers and from those who controlled public policy than did the men and women who used these mechanisms. Thus until about 1850 the adoration of machinery caused a fatalism which asserted that the best policy was to have no policy with regard to the relations between men.

The democratic ideal, however, operative in the past fifty years chiefly in the political sphere, has also affected industrial life. In the first stages of the new manufacture in the early nineteenth century the struggle was going on against the slave-trade and against slave-owning. While Western Europe and Great Britain in particular was being moved by appeals against the slave system, a new system of organizing production, upon the basis of large-scale machinery and new power-supply, was being developed; and happily, in spite of much unnecessary suffering among the new factory-workers, they were not made by law into slaves. The conditions of the workers in some textile mills and coal-mines were actually worse than those slaves endured; but the industrial workers had a theoretical freedom and reformers soon contrived to abolish the worst abuses. The early reform movement which resulted in Factory Acts and Factory Inspection was largely humanitarian and not, in any correct sense of the word, democratic. It was based upon benevolence for sufferers and a vague discomfort at observing starvation, which was similar to the feeling against the torture of criminals. But the reform movement soon combined with the political democracy of equal rights in Chartism and with other inheritances from the idealism of the French Revolution. It is therefore not unfair to say that the actual practice in industry to-day, regulated by law and affected by trade unions, is partly the effect of the operation of the democratic ideal. Some at least of the improvements in the conditions of work since the beginning of the industrial era are due to the conception that the common man is not merely a tool for employers.

A new factor in contemporary practice, however, is quite recent in origin; and that is more clearly a result of democracy. It is the attention to the mental structure and psychological abilities of men and women at their work. The early economists blandly spoke of "labour", by which they seem to have meant the physical force exercised by persons called coal-miners and textile workers. That these were persons and not merely natural forces in operation did not seem relevant; for personality had no price, and passions were regarded as imponderable, because they could not be weighed in the rude scales of a grocer. Industrial as well as commercial and financial policy was supposed to be based upon knowledge of economic facts, which were natural results of contemporary habits; and the men who moved material or thought out schemes were not considered. But in the stress of the Great War in most industrial countries it was found that the spirit or enthusiasm with which work was done made some difference; and it dawned upon practical men that the psycho-physical reactions of a man or woman working at a machine might be as important for munition-making as the machine itself. Modern physiology and psychology were available, and in Great Britain first the Health of Munition Workers' Committee, then the Industrial Fatigue Research Board, began to study "labour" in a new sense. Not wage-rates, nor foot-pounds of man-power, but actual feelings of men and women were seen to be most important for the devising of industrial policy. The National Institute of Industrial Psychology expresses the beginnings of a new outlook on industrial problems; and perhaps industrial humanism will develop out of humanitarianism, when knowledge keeps pace with benevolence. The Industrial Welfare Association and the industrial section of the Safety First Association and the International Industrial Relations Association at the Hague are further recent indications of the consideration now given to human beings in industrial occupations. The study of "personnel" problems is now a recognized necessity of good industrial management; and although very few firms actually practice a new art in this respect, the new attitude towards industrial organization implies consideration of the common man.

Again, the growth of trade unionism is a psychological phenomenon. It is an expression of certain abilities of common men so placed in the industrial system that they react to one another in new ways. The trade unions began as small groups of men who knew one another personally in the same trade.

They were associations for fellowship and co-operation in mutual support and protection against the injuries resulting from disease, accident, unemployment, or death. In the soulless world of machinery men discovered the possibilities of a new fellowship. They applied to it the methods learnt earlier in religious sects; and they developed their own rules of conduct. The hostility of those who had political and economic power towards associations they did not understand, made these associations bellicose. In many cases trade unionists learned to hold together by facing the threat of a common oppression. Then claims were advanced and some were conceded. The scale of trade union organization increased and some unions became, in Great Britain and Germany in particular, powerful associations with members in all parts of the country. A new form of fellowship and new habits of co-operation had been established. The attitude, habits of action and general ideas of a member of a large union such as the N.U.R. or the A.E.U. have no parallel in history. There is sense of fellowship in co-operation for mutual benefit; and there is an increasing sense of the importance to the whole community of the work done. On the whole, therefore, in the larger unions and amalgamations, new psychological factors are at work of which the organizers of industry are compelled to take account.

Finally, the democratic ideal has been operative in the progress of conciliation and arbitration between trade unions and employers' associations. In Great Britain in 1836 the first conciliation board was formed, in the Glasgow pattern-making trade; and by 1857 there were thirty such boards in Great Britain.[1] During the latter part of the nineteenth century in Great Britain there was a very great increase of "permanent voluntary conciliation and arbitration boards and of joint committees unsupported by the force of law and dependent

[1] See D. Knoop, *Industrial Conciliation* (publ. 1905), and C. D. Wright *Conciliation and Arbitration*, Boston, 1881.

entirely for their success on the good will of the parties".[1] In 1890 the London Chamber of Commerce took up the support of voluntary Conciliation Boards:[2] and in 1893 the Report on Strikes gives a list of Boards then existing.[3] The increase of such bodies was rapid, and the success of their work, not only in settling disputes but in preventing the occurrence of disputes, was remarkable.

During 1913 as many as 37 new Boards and Joint Committees were established.[4] The Industrial Court Act, 1919, and the older Conciliation Act, 1896, gave the State a new function in assisting conciliation, and the number of cases dealt with under these powers rose from 11 in 1896 to 1,323 in 1919. Thus both by voluntary action of trade unionists and employers and under the influence of the State, co-operation for certain issues is being extended.

The methods developed have undoubtedly allowed a greater play, in the formation of industrial policy, for the experience of manual workers; but the two parties, which hold the field, still eye one another with suspicion. Machinery exists for adjustment of rival interests or claims; but the interests are felt to be opposed and the resulting peace is only a balance of power, with the threat of compulsion on either side, held in reserve. The influence of the democratic ideal, therefore, has been limited. In recent years, however, in fact while the State itself has been transformed from authoritarianism to service, a change has taken place in the human relations of those occupied in industry. The recognition of psychological factors in manual workers and the organization by these workers of their own associations have either caused or been accompanied by a widespread claim for workers' control and for a new

[1] *Survey of Industrial Relations*, 1926, p. 254.

[2] *Report on Strikes*, C. 6476, 1891, p. 48.

[3] *Report*, C. 6890, p. 322.

[4] *Report on Strikes, etc.*, 1913, p. xxxvii. The history of industrial peace as a section of industrial democracy has not been written: but abundant materials exist. A new collection of Arbitration Agreements, following that of 1910, is now being prepared in the Ministry of Labour.

"statue" for manual workers. In most industrial countries, and particularly in Great Britain, the relations between managers or organizers of manual workers and associations of the manual workers themselves are established upon a basis of personal intercourse between representatives; and these representatives already discuss general economic policy.

Autocracy or oligarchy, however, survives as the chief characteristic of the industrial system. That is to say, those who own capital, through their agents, the directors of companies and managers of factories, make the decisions as to what enterprises are to be undertaken, how many men and women are to be employed in them, and, except for some bargaining power of trade unions, what proportion of the cost of production is to be paid in wages or salaries. The argument here is not concerned with an alternative system. But even supposing that some power is retained by owners of capital, great changes could be made under the influence of the democratic ideal. The common man occupied in industry, who in most industrial countries has no control over industrial capital, might be given more scope to develop abilities other than those of acquiescence and obedience. He might in fact be treated as a co-operator in a common enterprise for the general good, and not merely or mainly as a tool for the enrichment of those whose capital he uses in his daily work. But for such a change to occur there must be a transformation in the generally accepted attitude towards industry. To-day all concerned, the workers as well as the managers and the owners of capital, regard industry not as a co-operative service but as a scramble for private gain; and the hostilities and jealousies which inevitably follow make democracy impossible.

The industrial system operates in these psychological conditions. Some boots and bread are made available. But the majority of the men and women engaged in the process have little or no choice as to the occupation they follow nor even as to the conditions under which they work. No reference need be made here to bad conditions. The point of the argument is not that some workshops are badly lit or that working hours are too long: the point is that, whether good or evil, the conditions are not controlled by the persons who work in them. And good will on either side makes no difference to the existence of autocracy, which in industry as in politics may be benevolent on the part of the ruler and acceptable to the ruled. Again, the efficiency of the process for making boots and bread available is not at present in question: an autocracy even in politics may be more efficient in producing physical comfort. The question is whether another system is possible which would not involve the subservience of many to a few.

The democratic ideal applied to the industrial system involves an attempt to make the minds, thoughts, feelings, desires of the men and women at work in the factories effectual in the devising of policy or the shaping of daily habits. It is revolutionary, as it was revolutionary in the political sphere in the eighteenth century, to suggest that even shopkeepers should have some power over law and administration. But as political democracy has not destroyed but has confirmed and developed government, so perhaps industrial democracy will confirm and develop industry. That is to say, the purpose in view, when men and women claim to have "a say" in organizing their own work, is not to abolish work or to diminish the supplies of bread and boots, but to make work more efficient and the supplies better. The complaint against the present system of production is not merely or mainly that the goods and services produced are not available for all who need them, but that in the process of production resources of human energy and intelligence are wasted. Such waste implies inefficiency in organization; and it is quite futile as a proof of "efficiency" to cite instances of large profits drawn from some enterprises which are dependent on slave labour. Immediate profits may imply in the long run exhaustion of resources;

and the argument against State or municipal services drawn from the suggestion that they do not "pay", is a superficial calculation in money arithmetic, not a proof in terms of economic policy. But it is implied in suggesting that slave-labour wastes human resources that a more efficient system will in the long run "pay" even in terms of exchange-value; and plans for reform should have that also in view.

The argument here, however, is not concerned with the detailed plans by which manual workers may assist in the direction of industrial services: the problem is whether the abilities required for any form of industrial democracy are available. If common men are to be more than tools, they must have imagination enough to face the issues of economic policy on a large scale, and energy enough not only to break away from an established dependence upon the judgment of others, but also to work better under a new system[1]. Such imagination and energy may be available if the existing wastage is stopped. Exhaustion makes it impossible to judge what abilities a man or group of men may possess in normal circumstances; and the wastage of available resources in human ability under the present system is very great.

That available ability is wasted in the existing system, there is at least one damning proof—unemployment. Omit for the moment the possible sufferings of the unemployed and consider these men and women simply as natural forces, available as coal or water-power is available if there is organizing ability to use them. Water running to waste, which might produce electricity or even cleanliness, is not so barbaric a sight as men and women standing about without work to be done, because no one can think of any way to use them that will not injure some few who have power. There are about ten million permanently unemployed in the chief industrial nations. Even as physical force, that is an asset; but when it is seen to be mental ability, skill, delicacy of perception,

[1] See J. A. Hobson, *Incentives in a New Social Order*.

subtle feeling, fellowship in co-operation—all unused, the efficiency of the industrial system is more than doubtful. It can mine diamonds to adorn vulgarity; but it cannot make available the energy or skill of millions of men and women now unemployed.

But further, standing idle involves deterioration. Coal can be left for a generation untouched. A man unused becomes less and less a man. Even if maintenance in idleness were genuinely granted, the mere lack of integration and the consequent isolation of a man unemployed in the common service of his fellows, are harmful. It may be supposed by some that the deterioration in unemployment, apart from lack of food, is the fault of the man himself, since he could be energetic even if there is no place for him in industry. But once again, we come here upon the curse of autocracy. The imagination required for doing things "on one's own" is destroyed by a system in which work is normally done at some other person's command. Besides, the idleness of unemployment is not chosen; and enforced idleness is almost as deadening as forced labour. The records of prisons show it. But in fact the deterioration of the unemployed and the waste of the abilities they once had are not due merely to idleness: they are due to underfeeding and to the gradual weakening, not only of the man or woman, but of the whole family of which they are parts. In some countries a small maintenance is allowed to the unemployed; but most of the ten million now unemployed in all industrial centres are without enough food or clothing. And the percentage of unemployed during the past fifty years, at any rate in Great Britain, seems to show that the waste involved is not an accident, but a natural result of the system of organizing production. That is the charge against the system.

Next to unemployment the chief obstacle to the use of available abilities is the evil magic in the pernicious belief that work is a curse. So it is in a great number of cases. There is some work now done which, if it cannot be done by machinery, should not be done at all: and to be compelled to do it deadens a man, makes him despairing, reckless, or inert. But it is not too much to conclude that some abilities are wasted by drudgery, if one supposes that the glassy eyes of a whip-driven slave have abilities to see beauty, which such a life destroys. Thus it seems likely that in offices and factories many abilities are being destroyed by conditions unwillingly, but perforce, endured. That is not true of the greater part of contemporary industrial activities; for a very great number of the occupations followed are actually enjoyable to those who follow them. Even routine is not objectionable. Repetition does not necessarily cause either fatigue or the sense of monotony, unless it is continued too long or involves too much strain of attention or physical energy. And in the non-repetitive sections of work there is still a very widespread sense of craftsmanship. Short of craftsmanship, the feeling of satisfaction in putting one's self into a piece of work, even if it be only the addition of figures, is pleasurable. It is, therefore, quite misleading to treat modern industry in general as if it were oppressive to the manual or clerical workers. Indeed, since the reform of the extremely long hours and very meagre payments of the earlier stages of industrial development, the greater number of workers seem to have more available services at their disposal than in any earlier time and more vitality. On the other hand, there are still too many occupations which are organized traditionally and quite unnecessarily in such a way as to be distasteful to most of those employed; and in general most men have abilities for greater or more skilful or more subtle and pleasurable energizing in the work they do. The reforms of the nineteenth century can be carried very much farther. The remaining "depressions" in the level of industrial or commercial employment and the drudgery involved in some occupations can be eliminated; and all industrial occupations can be made more beneficial to those employed in them.

But entirely outside the objectionable or disagreeable occupations in industry, an evil magic operates upon the industrial system in the traditional attitude towards all forms of "work". There is no difficulty felt about energy in games; but if the same energy is called "work", immediately men desire to escape from it: and the common ideal, at any rate in most countries, is to be wealthy enough to be able to do nothing at all "for a living". That is still considered to be the life of a gentleman. Now democracy cannot be established if most men are striving to escape from their share in the maintenance of civilized life. The doctrine that work is a curse or an evil to be avoided must therefore be destroyed. The alternative gospel, which must be established in practice, is that work is a service, enjoyable for itself in some cases, but in all cases to be welcomed as an opportunity for proving one's manhood. And by work in this sense is meant activity which aims at the supply of a definite need of other men.

It is always a question whether psychological changes precede or follow institutional changes, whether, for example, one can change one's attitude without changing the system within which one lives. But clearly that is possible in some cases. Great sections of modern industrial occupations may not give the sense of delight in one's work which the artist has. The unloading of ships, the management of a boot-machine or a cigarette-machine, the laying of bricks, the collection of refuse may have to be done with attention, short of enjoyment. But a certain expansion of abilities even in such work can take place, if the work is felt to be a service of those who need it: and short of that exceptional imaginative ability, great numbers of common men can and do feel in the present organization of work a pleasure in co-operating with their fellows. In order to extend that sense further and to make it operate more generally it would be necessary, first, to reorganize those occupations which exhaust energies too rapidly and to give security of expectation, which makes a man feel that his work is his life and not a mere accident of another's whim or of a momentary "boom" in industry.

But releasing more energy and establishing greater security would not satisfy the requirements of the democratic ideal in industry; for those employed might still feel that they were treated as tools. It is therefore necessary to discuss methods of giving the characteristic outlook and behaviour of manual workers some effect upon industrial policy. The basis of the new method must be psychological. The facts are undeniable. An occupation affects the structure of mind, and a shared occupation produces a mind-group having a peculiar structure of its own. Thus the coal-miners have one outlook and behaviour-pattern, the railwaymen another, the cotton operatives another, the dockers another. The mind-group, for example, of coal-miners shows a vivid sense of co-operation between miners and a certain obtuseness to outer influences; for coal-miners live in settlements apart from other workers, and all suffer or gain together in the fluctuation of their industry. The risks of their occupation are high: the normal life of the upper air stands in abrupt contrast with work underground. The coal-miner never sees the majority of those who use the coal he digs; and the user of coal never envisages the conditions of the service from which he derives benefit. Thus coal-mining produces an intense and narrow experience, set in a surrounding impercipience. The psychological factors which should be allowed for in the formation of policy are therefore peculiar. The isolation of the mind-group must be corrected; but cinemas and wireless may make the necessary correction. The representatives of coal-mining must be in more continuous contact with those of other industries; but centralization or national organization may affect this. A similar analysis would show in each great industry a mental structure, outlook, or behaviour-pattern, of which policy should take account.

Economic or industrial policy in this sense is not merely financial or commercial. It must imply knowledge of actual men at work and skill in dealing with them, exactly as policy in the art of government does. Policy, therefore, must be formed at least partly by the workers themselves, because they know best what they are and what they need—unless, of course, the assumptions of benevolent despotism are correct. In any case, the least wasteful method of organizing workers is influence rather than compulsion. As in political experience, therefore, the contribution of the common man to the system of organization will probably be both administrative, in the sense that he will feel responsibility for the maintenance and improvement of the system, and "legislative" in the sense that through specially competent representatives he will feel his group to be a force in the direction of policy.

Policy to which the manual and clerical workers can contribute is of two kinds, (1) managerial, and (2) financial and commercial. The proportion and value of their contributions in these two aspects of policy probably differ in different trades, countries, or cultural developments. In the problems of management, obviously the workers can judge very well the placing of machines, the means of handling material, lighting, sanitation, and hours. The expert, no doubt, is needed to give their requirements exactness:[1] and the other sections in any enterprise—salesmen or purchasers of machinery—should have some control over the workers' requirements. But in the main the organization of the work ought, in a democratic system, to be in the hands of those who do the work. The process of transferring such a responsibility from those who now hold it must be considered in terms of habit-formation, not of decrees. It must, therefore, be gradual and experimental.

Here, as in the case of political power, the immediate problem is transitional. Will new power be misused? Men who have been driven, do not move at all when they are given power to go of themselves. Limbs newly freed from chains

[1] See Sargent Florence, *Industrial Fatigue and Efficiency*.

are weak or stiff. Industrial democracy is a growth, not a conversion. But the mistakes which are made in learning a new habit are not proofs that the old habit is either inevitable or better; and the risk of loss is never an adequate ground for refusing to work for a greater gain. Many firms are already making provision in order to create an interest among the workers in the efficiency of the work done. Rewards are offered for new ideas. Funds are supplied in order to support the worker who may have to be dismissed from his work and to assist him in obtaining other work.[1] Permanent appointment with pensions is granted to a quarter of the workers employed in some works.[2] There are attempts in profit-sharing and co-partnership, which are not acceptable to the majority of the organized workers, because generally the decision as to what shall be reckoned as profit is not in the hands of the workers in the enterprise. There is also a limited but successful use of works' committees for control of conditions in factories. And every new step made in the direction of democracy by the holders of autocratic power compels a new step in the direction of increasing competence on the part of trade unionists.

Thus in many sections of contemporary industry the workers already have some power of criticism and partial control of management. Small as these beginnings are, the contrast with the situation fifty years ago is remarkable. The worker is no longer uneducated or narrowly ignorant of the larger world in which his own occupation has its place. Men and women in mills and factories and mines and shops have minds of their own and discover ways to make their intelligence as well as their "labour force" felt in defining the conditions which they consider to be endurable.

On the second point of policy—commerce and finance—the workers have not so far secured, even through their trade

[1] Rowntree's plan for a fund which may be used if other employers take on workers for whom Rowntree has no place.

[2] Lord Melchett's plan of staff grade of workers for the Imperial Chemical Industries, May 1, 1928.

union representatives, any noticeable power. In Germany the Reichswirtschaftsrat has some power of suggestion, in which the trade union members share; but that is hardly a direction of economic policy in production. In very general discussions of economic policy, under the I.L.O. or the Economic Section of the League of Nations, some trade unionists have made their mark; but these discussions as a whole have effected very little. It is not, in fact, possible for financial and commercial experts to understand that a knowledge of the mental attitude of workers may be an asset even in a financial policy.[1] But obviously a revolution is occurring among the influences operative upon commerce and finance. Experts or authorities cannot now claim that no one else should attempt to understand their "auguries". Even the mysteries of banking are not regarded as the privilege of bankers; for the common man begins to demand that even banking policy shall be intelligible. Scepticism with regard to "authorities" is a preliminary step towards a test of competence which the common man can apply.

It seems hardly possible to say what form the institutions of an industrial democracy will take, if it arises; but social inventiveness is not exhausted. As general education improves and spreads and as organizations of those employed in any trade or industry become more powerful, the competence of workers in a trade will increase; and since manual workers are not hands only but brains also, competence to judge of commercial and financial policy will develop. This does not imply that manual and clerical workers will direct commerce and finance, but only that they will do as much as and better

[1] The recent Report of a joint Committee of the General Council of the Trade Unions Congress and Lord Melchett's group of employers had been rejected, in February 1929, by the two great British associations of employers, the F.B.I. and the National Confederation of Employers' Organizations. But meetings were afterwards arranged between these two bodies and General Council, and in general employers *may* be willing to face the discussions of financial policy by trade unionists.

than shareholders now do. The organizers of industry in a democratic system of production will be the agents and servants not of the capital-owners, but of all those employed in any given enterprise. Thus whatever competence the common man as an "occupied person" may have, it will be available for the general direction of policy. But the institutions for securing this may be of many kinds. It is improbable that they will arise out of trade unions, because a trade union is not confined to a single enterprise or even to a single trade; but there may be "shop committees" which will be the training ground for the new competence. And perhaps, as in political democracy, the sense of large units such as the city area, will be the basis for the grouping necessary in the formation of policy rather than the "interest" of a trade or occupation.

The first lesson of democracy, however, is hardly yet learnt by those who claim its advantages. The majority of workers do not understand the need to increase their own competence before their status can improve; and they do not grasp the position of the "expert" or specialist. For example, the majority think that they know how to do their own work so well that they cannot learn from scientific psychology; but obviously traditional methods may be improved by the elimination of wasteful movements. Scientific management, which treats the worker as a mere machine to be controlled by the manager, is obviously absurd; but movements rationalized are obviously an advantage to the workers.[1] Industrial psychology not scientific management is essential for the improvement of competence, which is the only adequate ground for democratic institutions.

But the transformation from autocracy to democracy does not depend mainly upon new institutions. New attitudes are needed out of which new institutions grow. And the new attitudes must be shared by a sufficient number to give a

[1] The Soviet Government of Russia has recognized this, even if the Russian workers in factories have not.

"tone" to social intercourse. The essential change, requisite for the operation of the democratic ideal and for the further development of the abilities of the common man, is to be understood by looking more critically and less conventionally at any product of labour. What, indeed, is the nature of a chair or a house or a portion of food?

In every industrial product is the blood and bone of the common man who made it. The clothes, the chair, the book, the walls, the streets—indeed, the greater part of the material structure surrounding the reader of this, are saturated with the spirit, the life, the feelings, and thoughts, as well as the physical energies of the men and women whose labour made them available. But it should not require much imagination to make the eyes of the common man, already sensitive to social factors, pierce through the "raw material" to the blood and bone hidden in the products of industry. In modern times the wearer of boots does not see the man who made them; but he need not therefore treat them as natural products of an impersonal economic system. Every man and woman in industry or commerce or finance is putting his and her vitality into the store of goods and services on which civilized life depends. The workers therefore are in their works, just as truly as the artist is in his; and men who make goods available should not feel reckless or apathetic about that part of themselves which they have thus embodied in service. On the other hand, those who use the goods and services so made available should feel in them the hands and brains of common men, bearing up those who use them. The immense store of human energy, upon which the simplest acts in a civilized community depend, is quite unseen by the individualist who claims a special reward for his cleverness. But a great change has occurred in the industrial era. The elaborate mechanisms necessary for modern life are embodiments of a co-operation between men that is far more intricate and extensive than ever before. Simple folk desire to return to the mediæval craftsman, making what is called the whole of an article! The *Mauretania* would take one man several lifetimes to make, even if he could acquire all the skill to get the material and use it. And in what mediæval back-yard would he build such a ship? Any modern is better than a mediæval product in so far as it implies that innumerable minds and hands have combined in a common purpose. Social co-operation in modern industry is never felt as a whole except in the envisaged result; but the democratization of industry would be promoted if more men felt in making or in using goods that each occupation was a part in the work of a team. The "division" of labour is far less important than the unity of the divided parts; for the division which the early economists noted has never been a separation of functions but a closer integration resulting from specialisms which have no meaning at all unless viewed as contributions to a single scheme. What the worker has lost, if he has lost anything, by the obsolescence of mediæval craftsmanship, he has more than gained in the modern experience of fellowship. Let his imagination, therefore, be active enough to see what he is doing and he will have the status in his own estimation which is the best basis for claiming its recognition from others.

That those who make goods available are paid for it and that they spend what they get—the dominant interest of economic science—is of minor importance. It is far more important to see that industry is a social service in the sense that a chair or table is given its shape by the mental activities of men, and in turn gives shape to the minds that use it. All goods made available are bridges over which one man reaches another: all goods are services and services are contacts between minds. Industry is fundamentally social intercourse.

Again, those who supply capital for industry, are serving; and it is of minor importance that they exact a price for the service. They or their spokesmen occasionally claim moral credit for the use to which their capital is put; but they are not in practice much concerned to discover how useful a service they can support. What owner of capital would take less on boot company shares, if he could get more in a diamond company? The Company Laws of most countries protect the shareholder from fraudulent directors: they do not protect the public from rapacious or reckless shareholders. But if the use of invested capital is a public service, the Law should organize it as such; for if capital is needed to supply the public with boots, it is a refusal of public service on the part of capital-owners to invest in tobacco shares. There might, at any rate, be some information given as to the comparative utility of capital in different forms of enterprise.

But further, if capital investment is a public service, it is so in co-operation with the manual and brain work which uses the capital in production. Therefore the owners of capital should regard the workers as fellow-servants of the public, not as their own servants in their desire to make profits. Clearly there is no moral objection to making profits as payments for services performed, however crude such a method of payment may be. And services ought to be well paid for. The servant has a right to that. But the dominant assumption in social life ought to be that the efficiency and utility of the service takes precedence of the payment for the service as the moral purpose of the whole activity involved; and therefore the capital-owner should be able to act on the assumption that his capital is mainly an instrument for public service. A system of production which is dominated by such a conception will be democratic—not because workers vote or careers are open to all, but because each man has a place in free service and all derive benefit from the organized co-operation in service. No man is merely a tool for another's advantage, and each is an agent of the other's interest.

On the other hand, it is said to be fantastic to suppose that men will feel about industrial services what they are supposed to feel about political issues. In the relation of citizens in a modern

State it is supposed that, although each rightly expects some benefit from his citizenship, nevertheless each has some conception of a common good to which his own good, at least in crises, is subordinate. But this is said to be impossible or very unlikely in industry. It is no more *impossible* than an international steel-rail combine once was; although, of course, such an industrial organization could not have been established by Pericles. Whether it is *unlikely* depends upon abilities which are at present unused; and they should not be assumed to be limited. The conception of public service and acts based upon that conception have actually increased so rapidly within fifty years that industrial democracy may not be out of reach.

The argument, however, need not be driven so far. It is quite unnecessary to suppose that men must become saints before incompetence is decreased or waste eliminated. What is in question is not a conscious purpose of individuals in an occasional choice of acts, but a social tone: that is to say, most men may always think, when they think, which is not often, of what they can make out of the work they do, and yet the social tone—the normal expectations of men, the current criterion of the value of an action—may compel a constant reference to the common good. The social tone will find expression in education for service rather than for private gain and in the standards applied by common men in their judgment of greatness among exceptional men. Already public service is accepted as a justification for certain industrial policies. This can be carried farther; and thus the common man in his occupation or in his use of his capital will feel that industry is co-operation in rendering service, not a scramble for private benefits.

CHAPTER VII

POVERTY AND THE USE OF WEALTH

EVEN the simplest economics implies that goods produced to be sold are intended ultimately to be used. The economist loses interest when the price is paid for goods or services; but there the trouble begins, because using and enjoying are unskilful. The advances in the arts of production have not been accompanied by advances in the arts of consumption, chiefly because the majority of men have used so much energy in getting power to spend that they seem to have little intelligence to spare for the methods of spending. The second part, therefore, of the problem of economic policy, under the influence of the democratic ideal, is the problem of the use of incomes. Is the common man capable of using his power to control services for the best development of his own abilities?

Only primitive minds will argue that the common man should be poor because he might misuse riches. The use of riches by the rich does not set a very high standard; and the argument would imply that if the right to riches rests morally upon the skill to use them, most of those who now have such power to command services should not have it. The most incompetent of poor men could hardly be more uncivilized, if he were given wealth, than some of the present inheritors of wealth. But paternalism in Communist and Fascist practice does seem to imply that the common man must be given "in kind" what is good for him, not money with which he may get what is bad for him. A ticket for the theatre or a food ticket may not be so dangerous as cash, which may leave the theatre empty and give power to wear decorative and "useless" clothing. But the democratic ideal implies risking the danger. Under its influence, policy would aim at a state of society in which every man would have enough to spend some of his income on what is unnecessary. Whether each should have the same amount need not be discussed here.[1] The immediate aim is not a complete reconstruction of society but only the elimination of certain obvious evils and the release of certain abilities in the common man.

The ability to spend, the use of the power to command services, is what is in question; and first it must be agreed that each sane adult in a community should have at least as much power to command services as will give him a normal human life. The existing situation distributes that power very unequally: and there are many proofs that wastage occurs, as a result. But whatever the good or evil in an unequal distribution of power to command services, clearly it is evil that some men, women, and children in civilized communities have not enough power to obtain the barest minimum of food, clothing, house-room, or leisure. Can their need be made into an effective economic "demand"?

It is sometimes argued that economic policy cannot "make more work" by turning men on to house-building, because such men are simply taken away from some other form of production. But whether this is valid or not, the same men can be used for either of two enterprises, one of which is socially better than another. There are two ways of transferring them from one to the other enterprise, from work in pearl companies, for example, to work in boot companies; one is by a credit policy, with which the argument here is not concerned; the other is by a distribution of purchasing power such that those who want pearls have less and those who want boots have more of the "effective demand." Perhaps only a credit or price policy may be effectual as a means of eliminating the wastage to which reference is here made—the wastage of human abilities among those deprived of human needs. But whatever the detailed economic policy should be, the end in view, under the influence of the democratic ideal, is clear. A social system is desirable

[1] Mr. G. B. Shaw's equalization of incomes in his *Guide* does not sufficiently allow for differences in the skill in spending incomes.

which is better than the present in this particular that no member of the community shall lack the power to live a normal human life.

In plain words, poverty makes democracy impossible and civilization itself defective. Poverty in this sense is lack of enough food, clothing, housing, education, and calm of mind to make human life possible; but the standard is not high. It is not assumed that normal human life requires much food, clothing, or room to sleep and work. A little may be enough. But even that little is not available for great numbers of our servants in industry. No complaint is made here with regard to inequalities of income such that one man has more and another less; what is complained against is that some have too much and others too little. And these others are not all incompetent or maimed or ill. It is indeed regrettable if the weak are unable to live at all, but the problem here to be considered is the problem of persons who are actually performing services in shipyards or tailoring shops or groceries or coal-mines, who are not paid enough even to maintain their efficiency as producers. The payment made, however, must not be stated in money, but in terms of food, clothing, and house-room. And the main point of the argument is that abilities required in a democracy cannot possibly be developed in any men, women, and children who are starved or overcrowded. Poverty makes reasonable voting and energetic work quite impossible. A man who is starved and cold and continually worried by the fear that he or his children may lack food to-morrow is not in a fit state to elect representatives or to use his energies in production, still less to appreciate music, painting, or the highest experience of religion. Poverty corrodes political life, weakens the system of production, and degrades art and religion.

But lofty phrases are traditionally applied to men for whom nothing is actually done. Poverty is an institution as old as war; and its evils are sometimes covered over by fantastic sentimentalism.

The worker in our modern world is the subject of innumerable unapplied doctrines. The lordliest things are predicated of him, which do not affect in the least the relationship with him of those who employ his labour. The ancient wisdom, as it is recounted to him on God's day, assures him of his immortality. That the divine signature is over all his being, that in some way he is co-related with the Eternal, that he is fashioned in a likeness to It. He is a symbol of God Himself. He is the child of Deity. His life is Its very breath. The Habitations of Eternity await his coming and the divine event to which he moves is the dwelling within him of the Divine Mind, so that Deity may become his very self. So proud a tale is told of him; and when he wakens on the morrow after the day of God, he finds that none will pay him reverence. He, the destined comrade of Seraphim and Cherubim, is herded with other children of the King in fœtid slum and murky alley, where the devil hath his many mansions, where light and air, the great purifiers, are already dimmed and corrupted before they do him service. He is insecure in the labour by which he lives. He works to-day, and to-morrow he may be told there is no further need for him; and his fate and the fate of those dependent on him are not remembered by those who dismissed him. If he dies, leaving wife or children, the social order makes but the most inhuman provision for them. How ghastly is the brotherhood of the State for its poor the workhouses declare, and our social decrees which turn loving-kindness into official acts and make legal and formal what should be natural impulse and the overflow of the heart. So great a disparity exists between spiritual theory and the realities of the social order that it might almost be said that spiritual theory has no effect at all on our civilization, and its inhuman contours seem softened at no point where we could say, "Here the Spirit has Mastery. Here God possesses the world".[1]

All this is not the result of cruel tyranny. It is the gentle oppression of an impersonal system, inherited and unconsciously accepted both by its victims and by its beneficiaries. The poor think that their poverty is in the nature of things, whereas it rests upon the assumptions of all those who take their food as it comes, without thought of the service which makes it available. And this system is universal and ancient. It is not peculiar to capitalism or to industrial civilization; for poverty is extreme in inland China and in the territories of Indian princes, where personal wealth is ostentatious. Poverty has

[1] A. E., in *The National Being*, ed. 1918, p. 66.

been endemic in all civilizations; but, if there is to be a democratic civilization, poverty must disappear. Customary and delicate oppression may be worse in the end than fits of cruelty, because it is more dreadful to hear that "it cannot be helped" than to stand up against a curse and a blow. But not all the sacring of evil by tradition can excuse poverty or prove it necessary, if men are really moved by the democratic ideal.

Some confusion is caused by kindliness combined with acquiescence in the continuance of the evil, which makes such kindliness possible; for feeling good is confused with doing good. Charity or helping the poor is dangerous. Nothing, indeed, should be said against the use of drugs for keeping a patient alive, while an operation or a cure is proceeding. A poor man must be helped, before poverty is abolished. Extreme distress should be relieved, even if there is no policy agreed upon in order to prevent it. But charity is no excuse for a lack of policy; nor is helping the poor any excuse for continuing those practices which maintain poverty. And yet there are many examples of the use of charity as a narcotic for the conscience of those who are not poor.

A great outburst of charity took place in Great Britain in the winter 1928–29 on behalf of the coal-miners. The Lord Mayor of London collected funds for them; the Government added more from the public purse: a fund was collected in Scotland for the Scottish miners; and after some confusion, the Government set up an organization for the distribution of these funds. Some reference was made to the parable of the Good Samaritan; but it was forgotten that that parable began with the phrase "a certain man fell among thieves"; and, in any case, clearly it would have been better for the man, if the Good Samaritan had come before the thieves stripped him. The outburst of charity only showed up more clearly the absence of any policy to prevent distress and the inability to devise or to agree upon one. Kindliness of this sort is probably an obstacle to consideration of the issues involved; and therefore, apart from its transient usefulness in keeping the poor alive, may be actually opposed to the influence of the democratic ideal.

Further, charity, however excellent, is not without condescension, so long as it is given at the choice of the giver and not as a right of the receiver. But very few, even in those communities which are believed to be democratic, understand the rights as well as the needs of the poor. It would take the argument too far for the present purpose if the shares of a shipwrecked crew in the available supply were discussed. It is unkind to say that music in the saloon is unjustifiable, if the stoke-hold is under water. But let a poet speak of the essence of the matter; for some poor men resent the charity which they are compelled to accept:

> The hang-dog fellow looked at me askance,
>   And shut his lips, mumchance.
> He said no word to quicken charity
>   But thrust his hand at me.
> No glibly muttered thanks fell from his tongue
>   For the poor dole I flung;
> But in his grey wolf's eyes was plainly set
>   His reading of the debt.
> They said: "Dost think, proud fool, for ha'pence thrown
>   To have me all thine own?"
> They said: "'Tis I that make thee charity;
>   Thou givest naught to me."
> They said: "In giving thou alone canst find
>   Comfort, in being kind."
> They said: "These ha'pence given, and thou art free
>   To lord it virtuously."
> They said: "What kingly right is this, to thrust
>   Thy fellow in the dust!"
> They said: "My right it were to spit on thee,
>   And spurn thy charity."
> They said: "I take it; but thou canst not lift
>   The curse that dogs a gift."
> This message in the grey wolf's eyes was set;
>   For so he read the debt.
> And I, too, looking on his hang-dog face,
>   Said nothing for my case;

But finger'd yet more ha'pence; went my way,
  With nought at all to say;
For there was truth in what the wolf's eyes said;
  And, shamed at heart, I fled.[1]

The argument implied in this undermines all ignorance of the right of members of a community to a share in the available means of living. The grant of a gift out of a surplus is not enough. And indeed, those who have any power at all would, under the influence of the democratic ideal, transform a system under which some are dependent upon chance gifts for a bare existence. But even the existing, if limited power of those who are not poor is not used to abolish poverty. Sentimentalism and charity obstruct their sense of obligation. No one, of course, desires to live in a society in which those who are now poor shall be maintained in idleness. The conditions under which the right to receive an adequate supply of needs can be claimed are obvious. Service must be rendered. Those who cannot or will not render service may be treated as thieves. But that is a different issue. The point here is that many who actually do perform services are not able to secure the right barely to maintain the energies required in the performance of their services. This is an inheritance from pre-democratic days, which the democratic ideal has not yet been able to eliminate.

Assuming, however, that the problem of the use of income implies that each member of a community has at least enough income for his needs, the further issue remains to be discussed—is the income that is adequate properly used? Not all the workers are poor. Many thousands of skilled workers are now getting, especially in the United States, more than enough for normal human life. The general rise in real wages since 1850 in Great Britain has been often described. Taking 1900–4 as the standard 100, then "real wages" in 1850–4 were 56; in 1875–9 they were 75. The increase in the consumption of commodities since 1860 is also remarkable, for if 1860–4 be

[1] Jean Richepin, *Wolf's Eyes*. Trans. by John Palmer.

taken as 100, then 1900–2 is represented as 161.[1] The general standard of clothing, food, and pleasures available is very much higher than it was in the middle nineteenth century. The set-back among some classes of skilled workers in Great Britain since the war has not destroyed the immense advance made during the democratic period; and thus at present there are very many workers who have more than enough for a bare living, at least on the old standard.

But, undeniably, the use of this power is not such as to develop what is best in men.[2] That is to say, democracy is hampered not only by conditions of work but by the actual incompetence of workers in the use of such limited power to command services as they have. It is futile to blame the capitalist system or industrial employers for the waste which is obvious in the households of workers who are by no means starving; and it is true that social life could not be improved by giving the incompetent more power to be incompetent. Clothing is bad; food ill-chosen and ill-cooked; houses blocked with useless "ornaments" and shut against light and air. Even cursory observation in any city area will show how many existing opportunities are misused; but a better use of existing opportunities would be more favourable to the prospects of democracy than a continual complaint that existing opportunities are limited. Defects of skill in the use of income undermine vitality, decrease perceptiveness, and thus repress or destroy the abilities of the common man.

Some attempt has been made by Consumers' Co-operative Societies to improve the quality and increase the supply of goods available for those with small incomes. And from the art

[1] See G. H. Wood, *Journal of the Royal Statistical Society*, March 1909, p. 91. See also Bowley and Hogg, *Has Poverty Diminished?* 1925, and Carr Saunders and Jones, *Statistical Survey*, A comparison of pre-war and post-war real wages, showing loss for skilled workers and gain for unskilled, is to be found in the *Survey of Industrial Relations*, 1926, p. 8 sq.

[2] For misuse of income by unskilful diet, etc., see *Reports on Diet* by Professor Cathcart.

of retailing the co-operative movement has passed to great wholesale purchases and to manufacture; so that the Co-operative Wholesale Society of England and the Scottish Co-operative Wholesale Society form not only important financial units but also leading examples of what can be done by consumers organized for the control and direction of production. Even here, however, the result has been only to secure a supply of standard necessaries and to increase the supply of goods in the current defective tastes. There is no sign that better designs of furniture or clothing are produced under the direction of consumers; but such defects of taste are clearly due to faulty education and an absence of standards of culture. Either better designs are not conceived or they are not skilfully enough presented to be attractive to a conventionalized purchaser. The Consumers' Co-operatives, however, have made the first step in improving the situation by eliminating sham and shoddy; and "good" products are perhaps the promise of beautiful products, which may be desired as soon as common folk cease to regard beauty as a frivolous side-issue.

Secondly, a great advance has been made under the influence of the democratic ideal in the provision of communal goods. This affects consumption or use in so far as limitations in individual incomes are conteracted by distribution of "income in kind" such as public services, roads, parks, and the rest.[1] What is called "free" education is, of course, paid for out of taxes to which under indirect taxation even the poor contribute; and such education is in a sense a distribution of income in kind. In a sense, therefore, the taking of education for his children is not left to the choice of the parent, if his income is small. But the distribution of income "in kind" by public services has not, in the democratic tradition, been an alternative,

[1] "Productive undertakings, mainly transport and public utilities, representing a capital of £2,750 million or £4,000 million, if we include roads, are already administered according to a variety of methods, all of which depart in some respects from the principles of private capitalism and unrestricted individualism." *Britain's Industrial Future*, p. 74.

but an addition to increasing income in cash, which leaves skill to be exercised by each man in the art of consuming. By such means, however, as public services, the defects of individual skill in using or enjoying services are amended; new abilities are developed and the taste for a wider life established. The effect upon poverty is not yet clear; but quite clearly a great effect upon taste is already visible among those with small and not altogether inadequate incomes. The demand for a higher standard of living, better clothing, better houses, more enjoyment, has been the direct result of elementary education and the provision of public facilities for recreation. The common man has, in fact, shown himself quite capable of appreciating more than his ancestors ever imagined to be possible. It follows that abilities existed for the better use of income before such uses were possible; and it is reasonable therefore to believe that still greater skill in enjoyment would be released if the power to command services were more generally available for the majority of men.

The power to command services, as the simplest economics shows, is partly dependent upon the nature of the services available and therefore upon the economic policy expressed in what economists call production. That is to say, the majority of men may have their "real incomes" increased by a decrease in the price of goods and services. But different countries and different groups in control of economic policy have in practice aimed at quite contrary productive systems. For example, the policy implied in making a small quantity of high-priced "luxury" goods is anti-democratic; and the contrary democratic policy involves production of large quantities of low-priced goods. The United States is very individualistic and, in that aspect of its life, undemocratic; but in production policy its controlling groups have been, perhaps unconsciously, democratic because they have "made a market" out of the unsatisfied abilities for enjoyment among common men. Movies, radios, cheap automobiles, baths, and household mechanisms increase the power to command services among common folk, whereas in other countries rare wines and silks and exceptionally beautiful motor-cars have left the majority of men in homes which are still mediæval. It is easy to point out defects in popular taste in America; the point is that the common man there has acquired some power to assert whatever taste he has. But the majority of the population in Europe and Asia have not any better taste than the American; they simply have no power to express any personal tastes at all. Thus it is possible, but exceedingly ill-advised, to contrast the vulgar taste of America with the taste of the select few in London and Paris, without referring to the existence of the majority in London and Paris, who have no power to show what taste they have. Indeed, even in London and Paris not all who have wealth are civilized; and the only proof that any are civilized is obtained when they have the opportunity to show that they are. But there is more hope for real democracy in bad taste than in no taste at all. Give men an opportunity to be vulgar and incompetent in the use of income and they *may* become civilized; but they certainly will never become civilized if they are given no opportunity at all to express their desires effectually. One obstacle, then, to progress in the art of using power to command services is the traditional flunkeyism, embodied in an economic policy which caters for the rich. There is, in purely economic terms, a vast "market" among the common folk in Great Britain, France, and Germany, not to speak of China and India, which the traditionalism of those in control of finance and of manufacture cannot or will not recognize; and it would not be surprising if the originality of American financiers or manufacturers, in such methods as "credit purchase" and large-scale manufacture, were to capture the market in Europe and Asia which the unsatisfied desires of common folk implies. No reason at all, except incompetence in economic policy, explains why men with moderate incomes in Europe and Asia do not use telephones or baths in their houses. It is customary, indeed, for advocates of culture to make a psychological "cover fantasy" to the effect that more mechanisms do not improve the type of character or conduct; but that is not the real reason for the lack of mechanisms in Europe and Asia. The real reason is probably a lack of organizing ability, or the running to waste of ability which might be useful in the various sands of a dilettante culture. In any case, the increase of baths and telephones need not decrease the production of good painting, music, or poetry, which can hardly be due to dirt and isolation. Democracy, if it is to allow a place for culture, must make that place in the daily lives of common men, not in "native reserves" where, as in Bloomsbury, the last ghosts of the eighteenth century may be protected against the type-writer and the vacuum cleaner. The development of the skill in the use of goods and services requires the removal of the obstacle which may be called flunkeyism both in culture and in economic policy.

But another obstacle to democratic progress is the actual extent of the power to command services possessed by those who have more than enough of such power. There are signs that taste is being hired by the rich; but the vulgarity of the desire for large sizes or large quantities still dominates the classes which delight to call themselves "upper". The complacency in ostentation, which is a sign of simple-mindedness, is widespread among those who are admired as successful. All this, however, is a cultural defect which obstructs democracy, not by economic but by educational means, which therefore will be discussed later. But certain incidental results of the mere extent of personal economic power may be noted here as obstacles to the freer play of human abilities. The "pull" of very large incomes upon the productive organization causes a supply of "luxury goods" and most of them are barbaric. The purchasing power of one man, exerted in the "pull" for diamonds and race-horses, might be used by civilized persons for discovery or the creation of new arts. Thus large incomes, which tend to turn production away from such simpler needs as would increase the abilities of many, do not turn it in the direction of fine art but of folly. And these incomes are hardly yet affected even by the high taxation which in Great Britain takes £50,000 a year from an income of £100,000. Even £50,000 left to one man is more than a livelihood; and besides, it seems waste of energy to allow the accumulation and then to subtract from it.[1] However, the argument here is not concerned with detailed policy. It is enough if the existence of very large incomes in a community, some of whose members have not enough for bare life, is seen to be an obstacle to the achievement of the democratic ideal.

An old-fashioned justification for accumulations of private wealth was based, not on the advantage of "luxury" consumption, but upon a supposed advantage to production. It used to be said that the "saving" necessary for new capital could best be secured if there were very large incomes providing a surplus for saving. That method is primitive and may have been effectual in primitive times; but clearly the accumulation of new capital might be made either from great numbers of comparatively small incomes or, better still, by large-scale reservations from the profits or surplus of industries, before any incomes are distributed from them. The existence of large incomes in any case does not secure that the so-called savings, which are really unnoticed surplus involving none of the mythological "sacrifice" of the early economists, are used in enterprises which are socially beneficial. Thus the fundamental issue is the use of income for public advantage. Some rich men understand that moral obligation; but democracy can arise in a society in which income is unequally distributed only if the general tone be such as to prevent socially wasteful expenditure by the rich. It will be remembered that during the Great War, when labour for national service was wanted in

[1] The prevention of accumulation by that most dangerous process, the inheritance of wealth, is contrived by estate duties; and new plans exist for a more drastic elimination of long-existent family fortunes.

Great Britain, a certain rich man had a private race-course built for himself. In peace-time that sort of anti-social conduct is common; and there is no method of preventing it.

In the arguments against democracy the achievements of the rich in earlier times are sometimes mistakenly praised, but generally by writers ignorant of the economic conditions upon which tyrants and courts depended. The Palace of Versailles is an example of an artistic product which was morally unjustifiable. Quite apart from the defects of the art and of the social manners which it expresses, the slaughter of workmen, the enslavement of the corvées collected from all parts of France, and the expenditure of immense sums in building the palace, were direct wastage of human ability such as barbarism could hardly rival. Similar balances of good and evil, with the evil now forgotten but outweighing the good in the record of history, can be found in the building of the Parthenon from the tribute of allies, the decoration of Renaissance palaces, and the deserts made for the pleasures of hunting. At least in our age the anti-social expenditure of large incomes is not approved. It is excused in the past only by the dilettante who has inherited the power to live on other men's labour. There is no moral justification for the existence of fine art if the price to be paid for its existence is the pain and death of common men. But the real issue is still more fundamental; for there is no reason to believe that what did occur must inevitably have occurred. A lack of social skill is not inevitable. It *may* have been possible to build the Parthenon without injustice to tributary cities. And in any case the achievements of the past are not justifications for the continuance of the evils of the past without any such achievements in the present. If great Art did occur where slavery was established, it does not follow that slavery must be continued in the hope that great Art will occur again; for to torture a man in order to write a tragedy upon torture is not usually regarded as civilization.

The defects in the use of the power to command services

are mainly due to a traditional culture or education and that will be discussed later; but another cause of the prevailing deterioration of vitality through misuse of economic opportunities is the current conception of the nature of an income. Against that conception the democratic ideal should be effectual. In the first place, it is seriously believed that payments for service are "rewards". The whole morality of reward and punishment is doubtful; for it is doubtful whether an act is good if it is done for an irrelevant reason as, for example, in order to avoid hell or gain heaven. It is likely that the only good act is the act done because it is good. But in the more restricted economic field, to reward a man because he has done what he ought in public service is either to treat him as a child who does not understand what public service is, or to suspect the incentives of other men who need such an example. In any case the "balance" is not completed by a payment for service unless such service is a loss to the servant; and that in a civilized community it should not be. Therefore payment for service is not the end of a process but the beginning: that is to say, one is paid in order to make one more fitted to perform future service. Income is a means for promoting one's efficiency as a public servant. What one gets for a lecture or a pound of butter is power to use services for better lecturing or better butter-selling in the future. A man's wage or salary is one of his instruments for serving his fellow-men.

It follows that the expenditure of an income is a public duty. The way in which it is spent should be such as to conduce to the general welfare. Some expenditure can be pernicious, as, for example, in brothels or drinking-dens. But far short of actual vice the democratic ideal involves that a man or woman should think, in buying any article or paying for any service, whether the article is cheap because of slave-labour or the service degrading to the servant. It is mere sentimentalism to say that one treats others democratically, if one simply does not notice the effect on others of the expenditure of one's own income. To buy a cheap hat may support a system of slave labour. To take opportunities for a cheap holiday may increase unbearably the burden of those whose labour makes the holiday enjoyable.

Clearly one cannot examine in this way every transaction in the daily round. It would be fantastic to make democracy depend upon so sensitive a conscience; and in any case the real issue is not the evil done by this or that individual buyer. The evil is done because the economic system promotes public blindness with regard to underpayment or slavish conditions; and the way to cure that blindness is not to ask the grocer how he treats his assistants, but to establish Trade Boards and the administration of Shop-hours Acts. That is to say, a general evil must be abolished by a public policy. The influence of the democratic ideal ought at least to make it impossible for any man or woman to say that he or she is "not interested" in politics or public affairs. The choice of a policy worthy of support may be difficult; but it is inexcusable to accept the benefits of a social system and refuse to consider the obligations owed to those who may be its victims. The superior air of a cultured and leisured man who has no inclination to be worried about those who serve him, is an extreme form of barbarism. Democracy implies civilized life.

But if the expenditure of income is a public service, then others derive benefit from the income of each and jealousy is out of place. Clearly that is the only possible atmosphere for democracy—an air which is clear of suspicion and hostility between men. And this does not imply that men will become an angelic choir. Once again, the point is not that conscious purposes will change but that a social "tone" will come into existence, when it is no longer regarded as honourable for any man to be a private appetite battening upon a private power to command services. But if each derives some benefit from the expenditure of income by the others, then it is unnecessary for incomes to be equal. The man with less, in such a society, would not fear to be pushed to the wall by the man with more.

The pressure to obtain more would not be so great; and skill in the expenditure of less would be honoured.

Secondly, the common man has a part to play in so far as he is a beneficiary of the existing system. Indeed, the operation of the democratic ideal would involve a revolution far more drastic than a revolution of the victims—namely, a revolution of the beneficiaries. Every civilization so far has had its victims and its beneficiaries; and the beneficiaries have always contrived to hide from their eyes the victims. In the city of Rome, which has survived two civilizations, there are two monuments to convenient blindness. In the Forum of Augustus is the great wall by which the Emperor strove to hide from those who enjoyed his beneficence the slums of the Suburra; and in the Papal Borgo the columns which enclose the Piazza of St. Peter's hid in the sixteenth century the slums of the Papal city. Nowadays the poor are herded in corners from which they and their children issue sometimes as strange sights in fashionable streets; for there are still in every industrial area two cities, one of the victims and one of the beneficiaries of civilization.

It is not impossible, however, that democracy will be taken by the beneficiaries to mean a revolt against exceptional good fortune. Not that anyone need be so insane as to choose squalor or starvation because some bear these evils. That is fantastic. It does no good and is often an excuse for sentimentalism. The delicacies and serenities of life are not to be cast away because all do not share them. But the retention and use of such power as a man has, need not involve blindness to the victims of an inherited system, nor hesitation to change that system even if by such a change some beneficiaries have fewer benefits. In plain terms, the democratic ideal would imply a social life more convenient for dustmen and shipyard workers, even if it was also a life less convenient than life now is for university lecturers and their audiences. And it is the beneficiaries rather than the victims of the present system who have the power to transform it.

CHAPTER VIII

JUSTICE AND WEALTH

So far the two spheres, the political and the economic, in which the common man lives, have been discussed separately. He has been considered first as a maintainer of law and enjoyer of liberties, through his agents, the officials and the representatives in assemblies; and secondly, he has been considered as the servant of other men in his gaining of a livelihood and as a half-conscious master of economic services in his cinemas and his tea-drinking. In both spheres recent changes have been reviewed. In politics government has become a service of the common man. In industry mechanization and large-scale organization tend to increase the importance of skill in social co-operation, and new forms of public enterprise tend to equalize the power to enjoy services. Both government and industry to-day are different from what they were fifty years ago; but a still more striking change has taken place in the relations between the two.

The past century has been dominated by the false idea that there is an inevitable opposition between government and industry; and many who claim to be practical men to-day are still looking at the facts with the spectacles provided by Herbert Spencer or Karl Marx. These practical men are quite unconscious that what they see is due to the spectacles, not to the facts; but it is useless to discuss obsolete theories, surviving in what practical men call their common sense. Clearly the Spencerian creed that the more public service there is, the less private enterprise, is quite false. It rested upon a false assumption that the extent of organized social life was fixed; but both public service and private enterprise have extended in the past fifty years. Similarly, the Marxian creed that large-scale capital organization would make the State the great Capitalist has not come true; for the function of the State in regard to industry has not proved to be that of taking over its management. Even regulation is not now what it was. The factory inspectors of Marx's day, good as they were, have been replaced by others who are not police officers but experts in industrial organization. The trade unions, which Marx omitted to notice, have grown to immense proportions and now fulfil some functions on behalf of the State; and the State seems to be transferring to non-political bodies at least as much as it is adopting for itself in the organization of industry.

The important point is that the changes of fifty years have shown, first, the influence of the democratic ideal, and, secondly, the point of advance for the next step in releasing the unused abilities of the common man. The argument above has shown how the functions of the State changed during the nineteenth century.[1] But in the process of transforming authoritarianism into public service, the relations between the organization for maintaining justice and the system for producing and using wealth have been changed from those of police and potential criminal to those of expert assistant and responsible organizer of the public service in industry. Survivals of the old system exist, for example, in the control by the State over the dangers of adulterated food. And on the part of employers or industrial organizers the old system is ingrained in habits which cause irritation if inspection is threatened or information demanded. But the new system is already established in some activities of government affecting industry.

Clearly the whole field cannot be reviewed here; for such a review would require an analysis of the relation, for example, in Great Britain between the City and Whitehall, in the United States the relation between Wall Street and Washington, in France the relation between the Bourse and the Treasury. And even that indication simplifies the issue; for the whole organization of government stands in relation to the whole organization for the production and use of goods. The point

[1] See above, Chapter III.

is that the two organizations are not now in the same relation as they were fifty years ago, although some old practices survive. Unintended results of the democratization of government are to be found among the effects of government upon industry; and even the very limited influence of democratic tendencies in industry has reacted again upon government. In both cases the common man plays a more important part.

The established form of justice maintained by government obviously provides the basis for economic exchange: and in Western European civilization the peculiar group of rights and rituals connected with "property" are fundamental. Ownership is a very obscure conception, referring to factors in social life imperfectly envisaged and still more imperfectly understood. But philosophy must be avoided here: and therefore it will be supposed that men know what they mean when they say that they "own" hats or houses or industrial capital. Now the ownership of wealth is no longer supposed to imply power to do with it exactly what the owner chooses; and the numbers or kinds of uses to which he can put it are continually being changed through the organization of government. At present some uses of wealth are absolutely prevented in civilized States: other uses are limited: and in all States part of what is owned is taken in taxation for public purposes. Again, methods of taxation now aim not merely, like tribute, at public income, but are deliberately used in many countries for redressing inequality of economic advantages in a community, or suppressing unsocial expenditure or diminishing inherited accumulations. Public policy in democratic countries seems to be facing towards a criterion of justice which will be applicable to the right of ownership, although clearly we are a long way from a practical rule that all "property" is a trust held by leave and for the advantage of the common man. Frankly, it does not seem at all clear that there is any sense in the phrase "public ownership"; but it may mean a form of organization which is an alternative to ownership, unless it means only ownership by a particular "many" which chooses to regard itself as a "public". However, it is unwise to ask men what they mean, especially if they feel strongly about what they say.

From the opposite point of view, that of wealth rather than that of justice, it is no longer assumed that government is a liability or merely an item on the debit side of the economic life of a country. It is recognized by those who are not still using their grandfather's spectacles that good government is necessary for the increase of wealth. If government prevents the use of wealth for the maintenance, for example, of brothels, it also increases the use of wealth by the provision of police to direct the traffic, not to speak of roads and drains: and if government taxes the rich at a rate higher than that of the poor, it is or ought to be positively increasing the available productivity of the whole community. But enough has perhaps been said to show that government and economic organization in modern life are not opposed but complementary.

A record of changes in government in Great Britain may be summarized here for the purpose of showing how industry has been affected.[1] Apart from legislation on banking, giving greater supplies of currency, there have been new company laws, directly establishing the security for capital-owners, which was necessary in the industrial system. Thus the State in company-law positively promotes the growth of the system for producing boots and bread. The work of the Courts of Law and the Civil Service is essential to the success of the system. Again, on the commercial side there has been an immense increase of the information supplied by the State on trade, tariffs, and conditions in foreign markets. The Board of Trade, Companies and Bankruptcy Departments, the Department of Overseas Trade, the Imperial Economic Committee, and the Empire Marketing Board, are new in the art of government affecting commerce. In all this government is not controlling those who organize commerce, but positively

[1] See my *Government and Industry*, for details.

assisting them; and certainly there is no opposition between government and industry.

On another side, industrial organization is concerned with the employment of men and women to produce goods. A certain amount of such organization, as described above, has actually been taken over or established anew by public authorities.[1] Great numbers of industrial workers are now directly servants of the State or the Local Authorities; and government seems in these cases to supply needs not supplied by the traditional industrial system, in roads, drains, lighting, and similar services, not to speak of communication through the Post Office. The State system, in all these activities, is actually an integral part of the industrial organization for producing goods and supplying services; and it would be quite impossible to tear out of the whole organization those parts supplied by Public Authorities. The State is a partner and co-operates in industrial services with myriads of joint-stock companies and strictly "private" enterprises. And all this is a growth of less than a century.

Further, in the action of government for the protection of workers outside the public services, a fundamental change of practice has occurred. In the 1830's this protection was secured by reports upon forbidden carelessness as to sanitation or overwork and by prosecution of delinquent employers. The early reports of the factory inspectors were, in fact, charges against current practices. The inspectors were performing a police function, and they were part of the organization of the Home Office, which is still in part a police department. But if recent Reports of the Chief Inspector are consulted, the whole tone will be found to have changed. The Report for 1927 put on record the "efforts of inspectors" to secure progress in the safety movement; the opening of the Home Office Museum is noted not only as a means for suggesting improvements, but as providing models for the use of those who are setting up new

[1] See above, Chapter VII.

factories.[1] Interesting developments of new safety appliances are reported. Again the Police (Miscellaneous Provisions) Act of 1916 gave powers to the Home Secretary to issue Welfare Orders; and four such orders were issued during 1927.[2] Scientific reports, warnings of dangers, and pamphlets with information on such problems as ventilation, indicate that the Department is no longer controlling or correcting, but assisting in the general improvement of industrial conditions, which the Annual Reports now recognize to be the purpose of the employers or organizers of industry.

The standard of working conditions in British factories has risen very greatly in the past fifty years, partly because of factory inspection, partly because the moral standard of employers has improved, partly because of the strength of trade unions, and very greatly because of the general education of the workers, who would not now endure such conditions as their fathers accepted. Naturally, therefore, the activity of government through factory inspection has changed in character. There are now practically no contraventions of the Truck Acts; in sanitation the higher standard does not involve more contravention notices; in regard to hours of labour there are no contraventions because the greater part of British industry is working for much shorter hours than the Factory Acts define. The function of government therefore has become a direct assistance to the organization of production for better goods, more efficiently produced.

But government has been extended far beyond factory legislation. The Truck Acts, Workmen's Compensation Acts, Unemployment Insurance, and Employment Exchanges are all now familiar. But it must be remembered that Unemployment Insurance did not affect large numbers until after the war: and Employment Exchanges began as lately as 1908.

[1] Such Museums had already been se up in Berlin, Munich, Milan, and a few other cities.

[2] Section 29 (1) of the Workmen's Compensation Act, 1923, adds some new powers as to first-aid appliances.

All this activity of government is still experimental. It is only in the past few years that any serious attempt has been made to train the unemployed, and thus prevent the wastage of abilities which might, if industry revives, be found useful. The security of expectation necessary in a democracy is provided by compensation for accident and insurance against unemployment; and the maintenance of a "reserve" necessary in the fluctuations of industry is provided by government. Finally the Industrial Relations Department of the Ministry of Labour, facilitating arbitration and conciliation for the prevention or settlement of disputes, performs a positive industrial function. Clearly, then, the State or government, with regard to industry, provides direct assistance for the prevention of waste and the fuller utilization of the abilities of the common man as a producer.

All this is under the influence of the democratic ideal in so far as the common man has been brought more "into play" by reforms. But still more significant of democracy is the change which is occurring among industrialists. Consideration is increasingly given in factories and in other work-places not only to the safety, but to the health and happiness of the workers. "Welfare" since the war has become a recognized part of any good industrial organization. Good lighting, sanitation, ventilation, and the avoidance of fatigue, by "spaced" spells of work, are all now considered, not in obedience to regulations but as a necessary aspect of the art of management. Industry, indeed, is regulating itself. The old police functions of government are becoming obsolete, partly at least because the persons in power in industry are themselves assuming responsibilities for improving everyday practice; and an instance of the interplay of the two influences—governmental direction and voluntary industrial reform, is to be found in the Report for 1927 of the Chief Inspector.[1] A draft Order for securing safety organizations was issued. Conferences were held with employers and the Order in the end was not made

[1] See Report, p. 15 sq.

operative because assurances were given by some employers that they would establish safety organizations for themselves. The need for some such organizations was recognized by those having power in control of the system of production.

The provision of means for arbitration and conciliation has always been recognized in Great Britain as the proper function of non-governmental bodies, the employers' associations, and trade unions: and there are now signs, as indicated above (Chapter VI), that closer negotiation on economic policy is necessary both for employers and workers. Rationalization, as it is called, involves large-scale far-reaching policy; but this is impossible unless the responsibilities of those employed in industry for devising and maintaining a policy in the public interest are accepted by them. That is to say, there is a definite tendency, not merely in rhetoric but in practice, to regard industry as a public service, to the organization of which all concerned must contribute.

But this implies conclusions which have not yet been faced. It means that industry is providing its own organization and regulation, not merely for the increase of output or wages or profits, but also for the development of the human abilities required. That is to say, the old police function of government is giving place to an autonomous regulation, internal to industry itself, while government becomes an assistance in management, as it has been from earlier times an assistance in finance and commerce. But if this change goes farther, then factory inspectors and medical officers may be industrial officials appointed by a central industrial organization. Laws and rules as to processes may be agreed upon by representatives of industrial bodies. Disputes and claims may be settled by industrial tribunals independent of the State, and there will be, outside the political machine, an industrial system of public service, establishing and maintaining its own government. Thus the pursuit of wealth will not any longer be assumed to be the only or chief preoccupation either of those who employ or of those who are employed, but joint public service through the development of the abilities of all concerned will be, at least in part, the ground of economic policy; and under such a system capital-owners, organizers, and manual workers would be able to play into each other's hands without fear that one group will take advantage of the other.

This speculation must, however, be admitted to be fantastic at the moment. The point is that industry is being democratized not by the election of a legislature but by the gradual transference of administrative functions from governmental to industrial bodies. Already Commercial Arbitration Courts provide for some needs of traders; the Railway Rates Tribunal and other such bodies are new developments: the "Safety First" movement and voluntary Welfare Associations provide new rules and new officials: and the continual reference of draft Orders of the Home Office to those concerned before they are made binding is a step towards self-government in industry. Indeed, those responsible in industry have learnt from the early practices of government that regulation actually promotes efficiency. Many obsolete ideas, indeed, survive; for there are still in existence old employers who disregard lighting or vocational selection or the dangers of fatigue; and many more, who admit the need for considering such problems, hesitate to spend money for future returns. But the general "tone" in industry is undoubtedly changing; and with it the relation of government to industrial organizations.

Democracy involves the substitution of the expert for the privileged person as the organiser, if the test of competence in the expert is the ability to act for the benefit of the whole of a community. Failing a "legislature" or representative assembly it is difficult, if not impossible, for the benefit of all to be secured. But pending the creation of some machinery for the direction of policy in the public interest, any step towards the abolition of privilege is a step towards democracy. But privilege of birth is being destroyed and competence in the public service given more weight, as an undesigned result of increasing the scale of industrial organization. The older fashion in industry certainly gave powers to privileged persons, sons, or other relatives, who may or may not have been competent; but family businesses are now survivals.[1] Something may be lost in the disappearance of small enterprises and of the intimacy between employers and employed, as something was lost when domestic industry disappeared. But the gain involved in large-scale enterprise on a basis of shareholding is the increase in the number of salaried experts in control of day-to-day policy; and these experts hold power because they have shown competence. The test of competence is still very crude—for example, the earning of profits or the increase of output; but the tests are improving, and in the very large enterprises it is becoming obvious that the tastes or prejudices of the consuming public must be considered. Rationalization involves much greater technical competence in the expert manager and a larger number of salaried experts. Thus a class is growing up which depends less upon the policy of shareholders and more on the public served. The experts of a great industrial or trading enterprise still feel themselves to be, not the servants of the community but of the shareholders; but that is an ancient creed or attitude which will become obsolete as the structure of industry makes it more difficult to maintain. The larger the service, the keener the minds in charge of it, the easier it is to act as if the public interest were the test of competence, and the more likely it is that some institutions will come to express the policy involved in this public interest.

So far the influence of the democratic ideal has civilized industry since the system began about a century ago. But the common man still does not play his part in the regulation and administration of the services he renders in industry. Why? It has been shown above that the principle of service must take the place of the scramble for private gain as the dominant

[1] See M. Dobb, *Capitalist Industry and Social Progress.*

motive in industry, if democracy is to succeed to autocracy in that sphere. But here the problem is the relation of the common man's citizenship in the State to his service in industry. In current practice a man is supposed even to die for the State; but he is not supposed to work for anyone but himself in industry. Therefore he is assumed to be at the same time both an angel and a devil. The result, during the recent war, was amusing, if it was not pathetic. Some men as soldiers were supposed to live and die for the community; other men as traders or munition-workers or ship-owners certainly supposed themselves to be justified in making as much private wealth out of the community's needs as they could. And this second standard was actually accepted by a Parliamentary Committee as inevitable in industrial occupations! Selfishness on principle never became so "enlightened" as to be a public service. Costings and control of material did not avail to stop profiteering; and industrialists learned from new mechanisms not how to serve the public better after the war, but how to extract greater profits with less trouble to themselves. Some may have been saintly and all used the noblest phrases, but the scramble for private wealth followed the removal of public control, just as though no one had died to secure the conditions of which surviving workers and employers took advantage.

The contradiction between the principle of co-operation and that of selfishness occurs within the blood and bone of common men. It is not only a division of institutions. Psychological attitudes now exist in most men which are irreconcilable, and it is primitive to attempt to adjust them by making citizenship correct or control the devilries of selfishness in industry. The better way is in accordance with the principle of democracy, which treats not merely every man but the whole of each man as potentially good. The common man must be made to feel that he should serve as a clerk just as he should serve as a taxpayer or a juryman or, in the barbarism of war, a soldier. Indeed, the common man was greatly praised as a "hero" when the sense of the community's need was acute during the war. But this same man is the shipyard worker, the tram driver, the grocer's assistant, and the clerk. And he is not supposed to be a "hero" in times of peace. After reading some articles upon the worker's "attacks on the community" for his wages, one would imagine that, so far from being a hero, he was a villain. But it is not necessary to be heroic in order that democracy shall be more closely approached. It would be enough if the sense of the community, which survives even in peace with regard to government, were stronger than it is with regard to industry. That is to say, the common man should feel his occupation to be quite as ennobling as his citizenship and the ability to make boots quite as much an opportunity for service as the power to vote. This would imply that the production and use of wealth is a part of justice, and good work in industry just as important for the good life as keeping the peace.

There is another contradiction, however, in which our inheritance of irreconcilable standards of conduct has involved us. It is to be seen in the relations between different nations organized as separate States, affecting the interchange of commodities and services. The problems involved have become familiar because tariffs and "free" trade have been discussed by those who choose to call themselves practical men. A practical man is a man who "practises the mistakes of his grandfather". But the argument here must not enter into the field of current political controversy. The problem is one of principle with regard to the relation of government to the industrial system. If, as was indicated above, they imply not opposed but complementary activities, government ought to promote such interchange of commodities across frontiers as will advance and not injure the production of wealth; and industrial interchange of goods and services ought to promote and not endanger the art of government. But in practice the common man, who desires more bread and boots and cinemas, is driven to deny himself some of them as a citizen because of the danger of war. He is told that he cannot afford to be dependent upon foreigners for optical glass or explosives or even food, in case war should cut off his supply. Thus the primitiveness of the State-system cuts across the natural growth of the economic system. And in this matter the moral relation of the State to industry is reversed; for it is the State which is the devil and industry the angel. Citizenship, which is a principle of co-operation within frontiers, becomes a principle of suspicion and injury to others across frontiers. The common man as citizen is compelled by the preparation for war to limit his "angelic" desire to see foreign films or eat foreign food, and to be an obstacle to the increase of wealth even for himself in order that he shall not also increase the wealth of his possible enemies. But the solution of the difficulty has been described above. War and the preparation for war must be abolished, if democracy is to survive.

Short of the preparation for war, it is sometimes argued that industry should be controlled by government in order to induce those producing and consuming within any one jurisdiction or State to stand together in the pursuit of wealth. The frontiers of the State, on this ground, would be made into economic barriers for the economic advantage of those who live within the barriers, and the economic community in this sense would be the same as the political in its membership. But this in practice is quite impossible for most States, because raw material and food-supply, capital and labour, are not found united within any State's frontiers. The development of international commerce has proceeded too fast and too far for the maintenance of segregate economic units which are "national". Nevertheless, in every community some services are localized or "sheltered" in the economic sense; for example, railwaymen cannot be under-cut by other railwaymen abroad, so effectually at least as engineers or cotton-spinners can. A rivalry therefore, within any linguistic or geographical or juridical community of men, may arise between those who work at "localized" services and those who work at export and import goods. Therefore a hostility arises, and the result is opposition between the policy of those who have nothing to fear and the policy of those who have something to fear from international commerce.

Those who fear foreign rivalry advocate purchasing only from themselves as nationals or fellow-citizens. They use the old suspicion of foreigners connected with war; but clearly that is not enough to induce the common man to buy only from fellow-citizens, in the case of lace curtains or imitation leather purses. He might be inclined to run the risk of losing the supply of these in war. The manufacturers of non-essentials therefore base their argument against foreign trade upon the needs of those workers or capital-owners who are our immediate neighbours. It is natural to wish to assist one's friends and relations; and it is also natural to treat as one's friends those whom one can understand. Therefore, one may prefer to buy bad boots made by a neighbour rather than good boots made by foreigners. One may prefer to buy something to drink from a man who calls it coffee rather than from one who calls it "café"—regardless of the fact that these are quite different articles. But the desire to help one's neighbour is not a sufficient ground for obstructing the growth of civilized life, which consists in increasing the supplies available for every common man and the numbers of different sources of supply.

To protect the worker from unemployment which *may* be due to the use of slave-labour, and even to secure the capital-owner from having his plant put out of action by meretricious or ill-made foreign goods—these are legitimate desires, whether strictly "economic" or not. But prohibitions and exclusions by tax-schedules are the worst possible means for such protection. First, they do not protect, except for a short time and in respect to very small sections of industry, and secondly there are much more efficient means of protection. These means are (1) greater efficiency of methods and (2) levelling up, by international action, the conditions under which slave-labour occurs or worthless goods are made. Such means are reconcilable with a policy of peace; but the effort to protect by raising barriers to international intercourse leads directly to war and in the process limits the growth of civilization.

The tendency of to-day is towards co-operation upon an always increasing scale. That tendency is not altogether designed, still less is it consciously willed by the common man; but on the other hand, it is not altogether a "natural" force bringing men together, for probably the growth in the functions and area of the State as well as the growth in the scale of industrial organization are incidental and unintended results of a change of attitude or moral standard, which is itself only half conscious. The desire for more food and clothing, for security from famine and robbery and for regularity in one's daily work—these are psychological factors in common men which have been in part the causes of large-scale intricate organizations for co-operation in civilized life. But the operation of these factors is now tending towards international cartels and towards "rationalization" across frontiers. Industry, therefore, in this matter, leads where government must follow.

Owing to the growth of international commerce the common man finds his abilities more readily available and useful. The desire for a good meal is less likely to be frustrated now than it was in the Middle Ages. The skin is more healthy now that green vegetables and coffee are to be had by most men in all classes of society. Clothing for common men is better now that cotton comes from far than it was in the eighteenth century, when most men stank of old wool. More men think in cinemas than thought in mediæval churches. But this progress of wealth is also a progress of justice; and the common man, under the influence of the principle of co-operation, ought to be able to serve and to be served even by those whose language he could not understand if he heard it.

The common man prefers this new sort of life; a moral

standard is operative, which is quite different from that of the Middle Ages, whether in fourteenth-century Europe or in twentieth-century China. And incidentally, first, the scale of governmental and industrial organization has increased to meet the needs of the new standards; secondly, the relation between the means for securing justice and the means for increasing wealth has changed.

CHAPTER IX

EDUCATION FOR DEMOCRACY

BESIDES the political and the economic, there is a third section or aspect of the life of man in society, which, for want of a better word, is called "cultural". The State and its subordinate organizations, as well as the capital-owners' and workers' organizations have been discussed; but if a list of institutions is made, a large group will be seen to be not included among these—namely, schools, churches, and artistic and scientific societies. Thus if the subject-matter for the study of social life be divided in reference to institutions, there are three classes; and three main divisions can be made among the psychological interests of modern men, because schools and churches are clearly not designed either for law and government or for the increase of wealth.

The process for which all such institutions exist is education in its widest sense; and the development of intelligence and emotion which is usually called education cannot be separated from the play of what are called bodily and physical abilities. Health no less than mental training is a part of culture. The body is not a mere instrument of the mind; nor is the mind or spirit of a man an alien ghost of the mediæval mythology, inhabiting "matter". The whole man is both body and mind. Indeed, it has been well said: "the man who can see any difference between body and soul, has neither". Therefore the argument here must assume the close relation between physical health and mental development or between the institutions for public health and those for public education. In this aspect of the problem the common man is not merely the citizen of a State, nor merely the producer or consumer, but a human being in a world much more ancient than that of the State or the industrial system. This is the world of friendship or of love. And in fact the common man stands in such a world facing a universe wider than that of social life—of trees and stars, of clouds and winds. The institutions of cultural life may be conceived as means by which the common man lives at his highest point; because through such institutions men strive not only to be more efficient as citizens or as producers, but to be members of a community in which trees and clouds are fellow-members, in which also there are presences hardly envisaged but felt to be real.

In this aspect of his social relations the common man is a fellow-seeker with other men in the pursuit of truth or beauty. Here he faces what, more than any democracy, "levels" the genius and the superior person—namely, birth and death and the deeper personal passions which poets regard as life itself. Autocracies tend to forget that common men die; and that dying is not an experience which can be shared, still less transferred to those who may be clever. But the whole theory of man in society, as affected by the larger issues of human life, cannot be discussed here. Only one aspect of the problem is relevant. How far do existing cultural or educational institutions bring the common man into play? In old-fashioned terms, is the education of "the people" to aim at the creation of instruments for the command of the few in politics or industry? Are the three R's or their modern equivalent "education for industry" sufficient? Do they give us in social life all that we can expect to get from "the people"? On the other hand, do schools, universities, churches, theatres, cinemas, and other means of education in the widest sense, as at present constituted and with their present methods, provide us with the only sort of men and women which is possible? If democracy is desirable, is the present educational system likely to produce it? If the common man does possess unused abilities, will they ever be brought into play by our present educational system?

In the discussion of the abilities of common men such problems must be faced because, first, more than half of any normal community consists of children and adolescents. The common man is *in* these, at a certain stage of his development; and the relation of adults to children and adolescents is one of the most important social problems. The general tone of a society is formed by the methods or manners of adult common men in contact with common men not yet adult. To express it in examples, the mother who treats her child with extremes of mood, from a blow to a hug, flying into rages and then slobbering with emotion, is doing her part to form an unstable, excitable, and unreliable society ten or twenty years later. No schooling may be strong enough to produce a democracy out of children who have suffered from barbarism in their homes. It is therefore important for the success of the democratic ideal that the treatment of children in their very earliest education should be skilful. And that treatment is in the hands of the common man.

Again, if the best part of the common man develops in co-operation with his fellows, as the argument showed above in relation to politics and economic life, then the habit of co-operation must be formed before the children of a community take their places in politics and industry. Democracy cannot depend upon conversion. Habit ingrained and not revivalist enthusiasm is its proper basis. But most habits are formed in childhood or youth. Therefore the necessary habits of a democratic society must be established among children in homes and schools; for it is unreasonable to expect those who are educated as egoists and self-centred individualists suddenly to become citizens aware of the public good. Again, in terms of daily experience, the well-to-do and the poor have different problems in the same task. The child in a well-to-do house tends to be waited upon and to regard himself as naturally a recipient of service, without rendering service. The child in the poor one-roomed or two-roomed lodging tends to regard himself as the victim of the existing system. How, then, can such children learn to co-operate in the common task of maintaining and developing the system? An experience of rendering and receiving service even in childhood must be the basis for a true democracy.

Again, the kind of schools and the subjects and methods suitable for an autocracy would naturally be different from that kind which is suitable for a democratic society. In an autocracy or oligarchy there are some schools for a governing class and other schools for their instruments. The schools for the governing class may very well be dominated by the "classical" culture of a slave civilization, whereas the schools for their subjects would naturally teach "useful arts" and a reverential spirit. But all former civilizations have been undemocratic; and therefore in many countries, and in Great Britain especially, those who have inherited some culture tend to believe that democracy has no connection with civilized life and may even be dangerous for it, although it may redress some grievances of the necessary victims of culture. The problem of democracy, therefore, in regard to education is sometimes phrased as though it were a question whether a democratic education would depress the level of culture. But those who so phrase the problem generally have in mind as a "level of culture" the very peculiar classicism of a governing or "upper" class in an undemocratic society; and it is indeed quite possible that no democratic system of education could produce the British "public school" and "ancient University" type. It is unlikely that it would produce Louis XV of France or Charles II of England, or even others! But the problem of education under the influence of the democratic ideal is not how to produce copies of an ancient pattern, but how to produce the common man alive at all points, vigorous in his interests, capable of co-operating with his fellows in the control of public affairs and the services required by a civilization such as never existed before. It is an entirely new problem in education; but it has already, in certain countries, been faced and a beginning of a solution has been made.

The facts of recent history must be considered; and for the

purpose of the argument, physical health may be considered first, and afterwards mental training. The transformation wrought by public health organization in less than a generation is altogether to the credit of the democratic ideal. Where that ideal has operated, disease has decreased, the death-rate has been reduced, and the length of human life increased. All this has been due to combining a knowledge of science and skill in the art of medicine with administration. The work of Sir Edwin Chadwick is already well known. Drainage and water supply are now taken for granted, although they have hardly yet been understood in countries outside the democratic tradition; but it is enough for the present argument to give some indications of very recent results in public health.

In England and Wales in the years 1841–50, the death-rate was 22·4 per 1,000 living, and the deaths of children under one year was 153 per 1,000 born. In 1901–10 these figures had fallen to 15·4 and 128; and in 1925 to 12·4 and 75. The mortality from typhus in 1870–4 was 92 per million; in 1875–9, it was 42; in 1890–4 it was 4, and in 1896–9 just over 1 per million.[1] In the city of Glasgow the expectation of life at birth increased from the years 1881–90 to the years 1920–2 by 13·23 years in the case of men and by 14·50 in the case of women. "Had deaths continued at the same rate as during the decade 1881–90 the number in Glasgow during 1927 would have been almost 12,000 more than those actually recorded. Life in the same period has been extended by about fourteen years, while the number of persons now surviving to 55 years is greater than the number which a generation ago attained 35 years."[2] The child's life has been made happier and more vigorous by the feeding of school-children, in some cases the supply of clothing and continuous medical inspection.

[1] Registrar-General, *Statistical Statement and Report of the Chief Medical Officer, 1927*; cf. also *The Balance of Births and Deaths*, vol. i, N. and W. Europe, by R. R. Kucynski, 1928.

[2] Résumé of Work of Public Health Department of Glasgow, 1927–8.

Whereas thirty or forty years ago the health inspector had to look for skin diseases and dangerous infections, now he has generally to attend only to minor defects of eyes or teeth—and this again not in all countries, but only in those of the democratic tradition.

The effect of all this is not only longer life but much greater energy during life; for the vitality of the modern community is obviously much greater than that of earlier times. Not that living men are more muscular, since the survivors of mediæval plagues were probably better beasts of burden; but vitality means variety and intricacy of reactions, and that, in a modern population, is obviously greater than ever before. It is sometimes said that the weaklings are preserved by public health systems; and clearly the policy of birth-control, that is to say conscious and deliberate choice by parents as to the number of children they will have, must be the complement of a reduction of infant mortality. But it is absurd to be alarmed now on the ground that weaklings survive; and most of those who raise the alarm are not honest. The complaint against public health systems is based upon the desire to save money, not to kill the unfit; for it is the plainest nonsense to suppose that a modern population shows more unfit children, diseased, maimed, or imbecile adults, than a population in the Middle Ages or the eighteenth century. Actual illustrations of contemporary life in those days prove the contrary. The cripples and the diseased in non-democratic countries are still there to prove what public health organization has done elsewhere.

In the education of intelligence two changes are recent—first, the extension of elementary education to all social classes, and secondly, the still more recent introduction of a new method, less bookish and altogether more humane. Again, it should be noted that these changes have occurred in countries of the democratic tradition—in the Anglo-Saxon, Teutonic, and Scandinavian countries; for although France has had education widely spread, it is still bookish there; and in other

Latin countries, under an authoritarian tradition, education is by no means general and the methods are still primitive.[1] The spread of education hardly began before about 1850. In former centuries it was regarded as useful only for the ruling classes; but since 1872 in Great Britain it has been compulsory in law, and, what is far more important, available in schools for all children. At present about ninety-five out of every hundred children of school-age are in the schools provided by public authorities. But this is so new in human history that its effects have hardly yet begun to be felt in politics, industry, or general culture. There are still men and women alive, even in democratic countries, who had little or no schooling; and obviously, there are many for whose education the early attempts at schooling half a century ago and the unskilful methods then used were quite ineffectual. Thus it is futile to complain of the limited education among the majority of voters or workers. There is no evidence yet in any country to show what an educated population would be like; but every year of the operation of the democratic ideal, extends the evidence on which faith in it depends.

The situation is still more remarkable, however, if the old educational method and the new are contrasted. A revolution has occurred within the last twenty or thirty years. The old formalism, "payment by results", the nagging inspector, the repetition of meaningless information—all these are rapidly disappearing. In the elementary schools of to-day there is music and dancing: history is dramatized and geography humanized; "arithmetic" is being replaced by mathematics; and the whole atmosphere of punishment and monotony is being transformed by interest in what is being done. Classes

[1] Compulsory education exists by law in many countries—for example, in South America; but as there were not enough schools or teachers the law is a dead letter. In Spain not half the population of school age ever goes to school: and most of those who do go to school are trained by Religious Orders to be "authorities" for peasants and other workers whose ignorance is regarded as an advantage, if not positively a virtue.

are still too large, and the school-leaving age too low, but the transformation has affected most of the public educational systems.[1] The results can hardly yet be estimated; but clearly the education of to-day will produce quite a different type of common man than the majority of to-day. It is not that the generation trained in the new methods will know more; nor that they will be more virtuous or hard working. That is not the point. They will, however, be considerably more interested in a variety of activities and much more subtle in their judgments of persons. Who can deny that they may also be less gullible? The modern method of education depends much more than the old upon social activities of groups of children, by which they learn the democratic art of co-operation; and in such an art they discover tests of personality which cannot be learnt from books.

The achievements of the recent past in public health and education are only beginnings; but it must be admitted that, so far, they have not produced the finer flowers of civilized life. Clearly some of the health and education which has been given has been misused; for Caliban often survives even after the rule of Prospero. In the *Tempest*, Prospero says to Caliban:

> When thou didst not, savage,
> Know thine own meaning, . . .
> . . . I endowed thy purposes
> With words to make them known.

And Caliban replies:

> You taught me language, and my profit on't
> Is, I know how to curse. The red plague rid you
> For learning me your language.

Education is indeed used by some in order to read the betting news and health in order to hold more strong drink. But to

[1] It should be noted that the surviving educational institutions of the pre-democratic era have made practically no advances in method; and when they have made advances they have imitated the methods used in the elementary schools.

take the limitations of Caliban for the essential characteristics of democracy is quite unfair. First, Caliban is a survival from autocracy. There are specimens of him in Petronius's *Satyricon*. Secondly, the ideal of democracy does not imply the counting of heads, irrespective of their contents. Even if there are more Calibans than Prosperos, it is not democratic to be ruled by Calibans.[1] The defect of Caliban is that he cannot bring into play all his possible abilities; and the argument here goes to show that democracy is precisely this bringing into play of all abilities in all men. But the charge against the inhabitants of democratic countries is not altogether false; there are indeed great numbers of common men who, although healthier and more skilled in reading than their forefathers, are at a very low level in civilized life. The problem is whether they can be raised from that level by any other than an autocratic or authoritarian system.

The acceptance of the democratic ideal as valid implies that it is not contradictory to look to the common man for the improvement of politics, industry, and social culture and at the same time to admit that the actual common man is gullible, barbaric, and unstable. This is contradictory only if what has come out of the common man is all that can be expected to come. But if the modern Caliban has power, it must not be forgotten that he had predecessors with still more power. In earlier non-democratic times those who were given or took power were not indeed elected nor in any sense chosen by the common man and they were very much more harmful for social life than modern elected representatives. Here and there a powerful person was also able and benevolent. That is so even to-day; but in general the king's favourites or the descendants of nobles were both incompetent and selfish. Instances are Madame du Barri's power under Louis XV and the founding of some present noble families of Great Britain by the mistresses

[1] Renan's *Caliban* is an unfair attack on democracy, although it is a biting criticism of actual political practice.

of Charles II. The choice of those who were to have social power was made by the sexual appetites of half-educated monarchs; and it is hardly possible to prefer these methods of selection to the undeniably crude method of popular voting. But the most fantastic nonsense is apparently still believed about the grand monarchs of the pre-democratic era.[1]

The positive indication that democracy is a better system than autocracy for eliminating the control of Caliban is to be found in the actual social customs of to-day among common men. Manners are better, social ease more obvious, cleanliness and grace of form more frequent in our streets and shops than they were in eighteenth-century drawing-rooms. The forms of social intercourse are less intricate, but the skill in conversation much greater. The evidence is to be found in the drama of the two ages. And the level of the lowest Caliban of to-day—omitting abnormalities and crime—is much higher than that of the nobles who sat watching the disembowelling at public executions not long ago. The truth is that the attack on democratic countries on the ground that the general level of culture is lower than under autocracies is either dishonest or else, as in most cases it appears to be, due to ignorance. The progress made during the past fifty years is by no means complete; for the vices of barbarism, such as drunkenness, still exist.[2] But the whole "tone" of social intercourse has been raised; and there is a far greater proportion in any democratic society than ever before, of men and women actively interested in the finer and more subtle human activities. It would be impolite to press the contrast with countries in which the democratic ideal has *not* been operative. The figures of the death-rate and disease-rate in such countries are available. Under the most benign authoritarianism children die to-day as they did in the Middle Ages, and men's lives are shorter and more diseased than under

[1] Cf. Bertrand, *Louis XIV*, with its skilful omission of the darker shadows, and the counterblast *Le Renvers d'une grande Siècle*.

[2] See Sir A. Newsholme, *Health Problems in Organized Society*, 1927.

the much criticized parliamentary régime. In many countries which have no voting by common men, the authority of the few has kept the majority barbaric in their amusements and inert in their work unless they are driven. In Europe and South America there are examples, and in Asia startling examples of the good old method of cultured aristocracy, dependent upon a primitive populace; but the cultured, too, die there more easily and sooner than under democracy.

The success of the democratic ideal in physical and mental development has been due to equalizing the opportunities of all men for health and knowledge; but the ideal has been often misinterpreted. The equalization of educational opportunities does not involve that every child shall have the same education or that all should go to secondary schools and universities. It involves only that the test for opportunity to use such institutions should be, not birth, nor wealth, but competence. Indeed, possibly a more democratic society would allow fewer entries into universities than at present, if its tests of competence were more exacting. For the ideal is not a society, all of whose members are equally foolish. If that were a democratic society, then a flock of sheep would be the ideal; but, on the contrary, democracy is a system of co-operation between very different men and women, and therefore the differentiation of competence must be more skilful than it now is. The youthful flock to Universities in some countries largely because a certain social prestige attaches to them; but there is no reason why in a democratic society a dustman should not have as much prestige as a teacher. The problem of exceptional ability is discussed later. Here the argument refers to the so-called "average" in each profession or occupation; and of these the training for one form of social service should be no more honoured than for another. The Universities are not institutions for training in all forms of service; and the most dangerous effect of a false conception of democratic equality in education is the "levelling down" which takes place when great numbers attempt to use instruments which they are incompetent to use with advantage.

A second misinterpretation of democracy is to imagine that it aims at making men's abilities equal. It is true that in societies calling themselves democratic, there has been a certain tendency to "level down". That is to say, there has been a popular suspicion of exceptional ability. Some have foolishly argued as if democracy meant that any man was equally fit to perform any function; but that is a *reductio ad absurdum*. No shipwright believes that a university lecturer can be a good shipwright. The suspicion of exceptional ability, however, is undeniable and especially in small groups where the ability can be tested. The less excellent shipwright is probably hostile to the more excellent.

A quite obvious psychological explanation can be given of the existing suspicion of exceptional ability among common men; for it is not natural or inevitable in a democratic society, but is an inheritance due to bitter experience. The common man quite reasonably suspects that he will lose whenever exceptional ability is given free play, but *solely because of the gospel of selfishness* which has dominated the nineteenth century. So long as each man with exceptional ability feels that he can take for himself every advantage he can derive from his ability, so long is it democratic to "level down". But it may also be *good* to level down for such reasons. There is a dim sense in the common man that abilities involve social obligations. It is not mere jealousy of the successful to dislike the clever rogue; and it is simply not true that the common man derives benefit from any "hidden hand", if those who have ability seize all they can of wealth or power. Democracy is not merely equal chances in a game of grab, although this seems to be believed in some circles in America and Great Britain. Individual liberty to take what a man's better brains make him able to take, is violently opposed to democracy. There is no real democracy except social democracy; not because one ought to "love" others—but because to neglect the interest of others in the proceeds of one's own ability is to be blind in one's own perceptiveness of social facts and therefore to be undeveloped. No man's abilities have free play unless in fact they play into the hands of other men; but the doctrine that exceptional ability is rightly used for private gain and is *not* an advantage to others naturally makes these others wish to level it down.

If, however, each man with any ability felt that his ability should be of direct benefit to others; and if these others felt that they might expect benefit from those with exceptional ability—then there would be no admiration for mediocrity and no fear of genius, felt by common men. The crucial issue for the future of democracy, therefore, is the conduct of those who have exceptional ability; but that must be discussed later.

Whatever the obligations of those who have exceptional ability, the common man needs to be much more skilful in recognizing differences of ability. The progress of education for a democratic state of society requires much more attention to the training of skill in social intercourse. In spite of the very great advance made in methods in the past twenty years, schools are still too much influenced by the obsolete ideal of individualistic egoism. They tend to train each one alone, in competition with others. The examination system and even the modern intelligence tests are individualistic, in the sense that they both assume the person tested to be isolated from all assistance. There are no genuine group tests, such as would show how quickly or easily children can play into one another's hands in the spread or the advancement of knowledge. Games and dancing are still more social than are pursuits conceived to be intellectual.[1] But a democratic society needs men and women who are able to derive advantage from the ability of

[1] This shows itself in adult life. The "workers of the world unite", not in industry, but at football and baseball matches. That is all to the good, so far as it goes. Rousseau had not as good evidence of the "general will" in a Swiss canton voting as a political philosopher can get to-day in a football crowd. But education might train for fellowship otherwise than in games.

others. It needs a much greater skill in intellectual co-operation than autocracy does. Educational methods therefore should be improved, with a view to increasing the abilities for social intercourse and co-operation in every aspect of life. Drama is better than class instruction. Speaking and listening are much more important than reading and writing. "Cribbing" is much better than isolation. Clearly independence and self-reliance are valuable, but not at the cost of blindness to what "the other fellow" is doing or thinking. The sense of fellowship, so widespread among children, is often destroyed by schooling or reduced to a hideous travesty of democracy in the domination of a uniform standard among a society of small boys or small girls. The respect for the differences of others and for their "place in the field" has not yet been adequately used in education. Education for democracy therefore needs better methods of training the young to be aware of the factors relevant to social intercourse and to be skilful in their use of communication and co-operation.

The common man, meantime, outside the schools, has a function to perform in his use of the opportunities for improved health and intelligence. The general education of a democratic society demands in the common man (1) social abilities and (2) the performance of some distinguishable function of his own in the common service. This should make social institutions "run". It should provide for the normal needs of a community—the milk in the morning, the train to the office, the meals of the day, the lights in the evening. A society of men so trained and so applying their skill should be as efficient as any dictatorship or aristocracy, in which the majority are merely instruments of another's will. But, no doubt, that form of efficiency is more difficult to develop and maintain than the form ready-made by a dictator. To the untrained eye the order in a democratic efficiency seems to be confusion, by comparison to the marching of a regiment; and it is indeed a difficult sort of order for primitive minds to grasp. Some mathematical series are less simple than the series of the ordinal numbers; but the more complex order is not less orderly. A democratic order will be a complex order of intricate institutions for co-operation between the members of a community and for extending this co-operation between communities.

It is likely that a democratic order will be *more* efficient than a dictated order, because more is actually done by persons who, freely and of their own understanding, play into each other's hands. The total result is a fuller life for everyone concerned. There is more vitality in the contacts of persons. But it is conceivable that, in any one very simple test, a dictated order may appear to be more efficient. For example, if all forms of thought are sacrificed to the running of railways, conceivably the railways may be more efficient for a time. If all chances of individual judgment are eliminated by a mechanism, conceivably production may be more efficient for a time. But waste is involved in all forms of the mechanization of men. As we say, the men cannot "stand it". And in the long run the more flexible efficiency of free intercourse and voluntary co-operation gives the best results. Results, however, of this kind may not be calculable in statistical terms. The greater output due to increased vitality is not the most important result of the improved health and intelligence of a democratic community. Far more important is the change in the quality of personal character and conduct, of social skill and of "good company", which is hardly to be expressed in a formula. Qualitative differences in common men distinguish an authoritarian from a democratic social life; and such differences should be promoted by education for democracy.

CHAPTER X

THE SPIRITUAL POWER

If the common man is capable of contributing to current policy in public affairs and of being educated to use more social abilities, he must face another and more subtle test. He must be able to control and direct the changes which are inevitable in any society. The efficiency of any system, therefore, is not its most important characteristic; for every system is necessarily in transition and must lead on or lead backwards. Time is real, and indeed so powerful that no generation can resist it. The State, the industrial system, the relation of man to nature—all are changing under our eyes.

It follows that life outside the habits required for daily intercourse is essential even for the continuance of that intercourse. Perceptions acute enough to envisage what has not yet occurred, sympathies subtle enough to forestall evil, and even a reserve of strength for action in issues which have not yet arisen—these are abilities required from the common man in the history of civilization. Again, the habits which maintain a system bring men up against certain obstacles such as poverty and war, which have been already discussed; and although such evils may not be great enough to stop the machine, a social system which provides for their elimination is obviously better than one which merely survives the friction they cause. In other words a progressive society is better than one which maintains itself unchanged, because the elimination of evils gives freer play to the abilities of men. Social evils, however, cannot be eliminated unless men stand at least so far above the battle of daily existence as to be able to envisage the transformation of what is customary. That is the meaning of the early Christian phrase—"We look for a new heaven and a new earth where justice abides". Finally, the strength for great social transformations comes from a fervour which has been called religious, that is to say an emotion arising from a vision of man in the universe. In such a vision the excellence of fine character or conduct, the beauty to be felt scattered among the factors of experience, and what used to be called "the divine" at once dwarf and exalt the life of man in society. And without some consciousness of that larger world, a community remains barbaric, however perfect its politics, however efficient its industry. Even education becomes only a trick for securing trivial comforts, unless the schools catch some light from a serener air than that of daily needs. The ultimate test of a civilization is not the security of its basis but the quality of its highest achievements. Works of art and types of character are the finest products of any social system; and if democracy cannot produce a better quality of these than existed in earlier forms of society, democracy may fairly be condemned.

It is admitted that contemporary industrial society is defective in taste and creative power in the arts. "Machinery of every kind you can make and use to perfection: but you cannot build a house or paint a picture, still less can you worship or aspire. Look at your streets. Row on row of little boxes, one like another, lacking in all that is essential, loaded with all that is superfluous. This is what passes with you for architecture. Your literature is the daily Press with its stream of solemn fatuity, anecdotes, puzzles, puns, and police-court scandals". Such is the charge brought against industrial city-dwellers.[1] And granted the charge, the opponents of democracy urge that ugliness and meanness in common life are the results of giving power over public affairs to the common man. The common man is blamed for degrading architects and poets; and democracy is supposed to have made fine art impossible, because public taste is necessarily bad taste. There is, however, another

[1] G. Lowes Dickinson, *Letters of John Chinaman*; but Mr. Dickinson does not use this as an argument against democracy, and he may agree with the diagnosis of the disease, which follows here.

explanation of banality and superficiality in a society. It is—the failure of the Spiritual Power.

In every civilized community there has been and is some force moving men more deeply than appetites that can be satisfied by goods and services. That force is called traditionally the Spiritual Power; and the name may be used still, if it is not confused or limited by obsolete meanings. In the European Middle Ages the Spiritual Power was the organized Church; but what was then called religion was closely connected with learning and the arts. The church-building in a mediæval town or country-side was the centre not only for worship or magic, but also for dancing, music, and such painting or other arts as were available. The *studium*, or mediæval university and school, was part of the *ecclesia*. In the modern world what corresponds to the mediæval church-building is a whole group of separate "cultural" buildings—theatres, dance-halls, cinemas, art-galleries, museums, as well as churches, schools, and university buildings. Thus the Spiritual Power in our day includes all those institutions which lift men out of the common round of habit. All means by which a community is brought into contact with beauty or new truth in discovery or new "interests" in entertainments—all these are the Spiritual Power. They are social organizations of which the influence is dependent partly upon the supply of idealism or insight in common men, but much more upon the use of such insight by exceptional men and women

This force, which shows itself in the institutions of the Spiritual Power, exists in the common man; for most men have a tendency to discontent with the established order; and if some men have no such tendency, probably grinding circumstances have obscured or obliterated what they had as children. There is, of course, a mean discontent, which arises out of jealousy or laziness, in the case of men who desire to get much and give little. And some forms of revolution can be made out of mean discontent. But this discontent is a shadowy substitute for the *sæva indignatio*, the noble resentment at circumstances unworthy of men, evils for which perhaps no one is to blame. The capacity for this nobler discontent is to be found everywhere among common men; and more than that—common men show in their discontent a sense of beauty and the divine, which the opponents of democracy too easily discount, because the poet in the common man is dumb.

Therefore a Spiritual Power is natural to a democracy. Men do not fail to distinguish one impulse from another. They know of themselves and without the assistance of superior persons that what happens to them at the sight of beauty is finer or more enduring or deeper down than what may happen to them after drinking whisky.[1] Quite ordinary persons—shipyard workers, textile workers, dustmen, and clerks, are moved by melody and colour and by the intangible attractiveness of a fine personality. That is to say, all men belong to the Spiritual Power. Clergy, teachers, professors, artists, and scientists do not *make* the Spiritual Power; they are only its agents and instruments, exceptional perhaps in ability, but deriving sustenance from the common soil of general human experience. The issues which reveal the heights and depths of the universe are birth and death and personal passion, which quite common men endure; and no genius can have more, although he may read the revelation more skilfully.

But this democratic interpretation of the Spiritual Power is plainly in the Protestant tradition. It is irreconcilable with authoritarian religion, academic art, and dogmatizing science. It implies that there are perversions of the Spiritual Power, just as there are perversions of government, and that the greatest perversions in both spheres are similar. But to say more

[1] For the satisfaction of scholars it may be noted that this is a direct contradiction of Plato's statement about the "democratic man". No common man, but only a lunatic, fails to distinguish the value of one impulse from that of another.

here would perhaps hurt more than it helped; for the main course of the argument is positive. There is a Spiritual Power which grows naturally among common men.

Further, this Power is organized to-day in Churches, theatres, and the rest, in which men and women claiming exceptional insight or status make use of what enthusiasm or inspiration they can. The institutions of the Spiritual Power therefore are the natural sources for what is finest in any civilization. The schools should produce more than citizens or workers: they should produce men and women of rare quality. The Churches should raise the level of religious enthusiasm or insight. Science and art, organized or in individual workers, should increase the range of human experience.

What functions, then, are actually performed in social life to-day by the institutions of the Spiritual Power? Clearly it is difficult to make an exact assessment of the excellences and the defects of contemporary churches, art schools, universities, or scientific societies. But to regard them as satisfactory would imply either that they cannot be expected to be better than they are—which is to insult them—or that the evils against which they might contend are of minor importance, which is no excuse for failing to destroy such evils. The ignorance and evil-doing and ugliness of to-day are tests of the efficacy of the Spiritual Power, and by no means adequate grounds for its priests and prophets to blaspheme against the common man. But the opponents of democracy are generally to be found among the officials or prominent persons in such institutions; and therefore, although the failures of the common man are not denied by those who profess to be cultured, any criticism of clergy, professors, artists, or scientists is resented by them. However, a heavy charge can be made against the existing institutions for religion, art, and science. The defects of the common man cannot obscure the no less obvious defects of his critics, who might be his guides.

On the debit side, the Churches in the Western world have

still to make amends for their great failure to affect the situation in the earlier years of the industrial revolution. The gross complacency of the pious among the beneficiaries of the new oppression is to be found expressed in Wilberforce's *Practical View of Christianity*, in which the wealthy author says that Christianity makes the inequalities of the social scale "less galling to the lower orders", and in Paley's *Reasons for Contentment addressed to the Labouring Part of the British Public*, in which the robust archdeacon shows that "some of the necessities which poverty imposes are not hardships but pleasures".[1] Undoubtedly the Churches were used as means to make evils endurable, not as instruments to destroy them; and it is possible that some boys' clubs and other devices are used even now for the same purpose. The failure of the Spiritual Power in the Churches is not an accident. Some vital defect in the attitude of religious men is suspected.

When the Church of England was turned into the moral police of the State, it lost the independence which might have enabled it to maintain the peculiar and distinctive Christian standard of social conduct. . . . Had the Nonconformist societies taken up the testimony which the Church of England had dropped, the Christian tradition of social ethics might have continued to find an organ of expression. . . . But the very circumstances of their origin disposed the Nonconformist Churches to lay only a light emphasis on the social aspects of Christianity. . . . Individualist in their faith, they were individualist in their interpretation of social morality. Insisting that the essence of religion was the contact of the individual soul with its Maker, they regarded the social order and its consequences, not as the instruments through which grace is mediated, or as steps in the painful progress by which the soul climbs to a fuller vision, but as something external, alien, and irrelevant. . . . The idea that conduct which is commercially successful may be morally wicked is as unfamiliar to the modern world as the idea that a type of social organization which is economically efficient may be inconsistent with principles of right.[2]

---

[1] See Hammond, *The Town Labourer*, "The Conscience of the Rich", p. 232 sq.

[2] Tawney, *The Acquisitive Society*, p. 229 sq. See also his *Religion and the Rise of Capitalism.*

Thus the Church, in the widest sense of that word, which is still part of the Spiritual Power, seems to have lacked the strength to resist the growth of economic and political evils, and to have caused its own defeat by implying that religion had no concern with what most men were doing most of the time. Individual Churchmen and small groups of religious reformers did indeed effect some changes. Lord Shaftesbury and the Evangelicals applied religious fervour to industrial reform; and recently the Christian Churches in the United States stirred the public conscience in reference to the Steel strike. Such institutions as the Industrial Christian Fellowship in Great Britain provide criticism of contemporary industrial practice; and some religious groups are concerned with more serious policy than providing comfort for the poor. But as a whole, if it can be conceived as a whole, the Spiritual Power in the Churches has lost all control of social standards in business or in politics. It is chained to the proprieties. It cannot "afford" to criticize the customary selfishness—private greed or national violence. And, indeed, it may have no principle of criticism, for the theological student and the future religious teacher knows more about Virgin Birth or the commentary on texts than about slavery in industrial occupations or burglary in the extracting of profits. When war occurs, the Churches hasten to bless it; and in the intervals between wars they "look the other way" while new wars are being prepared. Again, some individual Churchmen do make protests; but as a social unit the Church either has no mind at all or no power to express it.

This is not new in the history of Churches; and therefore it cannot be a result of democracy. Court preachers, of whom Bossuet was the most objectionable, for many generations before the industrial era, have fastened oppression upon common men by praise of those who paid preachers. In the far past there have been examples of criticism and condemnation of the Powers in politics and economic life by religious men. But the Church, as an institution or group of institutions, has long failed to affect the current social morality in public affairs. Is it therefore to be considered strange if the common man lacks illumination and cannot see "the divine" in the normal activities of daily life? The quality of what is called religion has been degraded into formalism on one side and childish revivalism on the other. But that is not due to the democratic ideal. The degradation is the result of the silence or the subservience of those who had exceptional ability or exceptional opportunities in the Churches.

Another section of the Spiritual Power is in the learned world of Universities and Scientific societies. They have done some good in preserving traces of a traditional culture in a world obsessed by the production and possession of wealth. The Scientists have discovered new mechanisms and the cures of some diseases. But the Universities have, in the main, been traditionalist, more concerned with Athens in the fifth century before Christ than with London and Glasgow in our own time. They have preserved an old culture—but produced none. They look back, not forward. And in the stress of modern problems they supply only platitudes or colourless formulæ. In the elementary schools, as it has been shown above, the methods of education are new; but the Universities still practise the obsolete mediæval lecture *en masse*. And on the scientific side, although they are beginning to be aware of agriculture outside Vergil, they seem just as willing to produce new instruments of destruction as they are to study cures of disease.

The Art Schools and Academies, from which might come illumination of common life, seem to be attempting only small tricks in corners, leaving the streets drab and the manners and customs of daily intercourse ugly and colourless. They have turned the arts into drawing-room accomplishments. It s not implied that the arts are merely instruments for social reform or for moralizing men, according to the Ruskinian Gospel. That doctrine is false. But it is true that fundamental art, as contrasted with the formal art of "superior" persons, makes men more percipient, more susceptible to fine qualities in experience, and more vigorous in their emotional reactions; and therefore indirectly the arts make men restless in the endurance of evils. In modern times, however, the effect of the arts has been trivial. Again, the Spiritual Power in the arts has looked back and not forward. The plastic arts, architecture, and the rest, have been dominated by the same Classicism as the Universities; and the architects and painters are only now beginning to handle new material otherwise than the Greeks or the Middle Ages or the Renaissance handled wood and stone. In music, happily, the Greeks and Romans left nothing, and therefore we have been able to advance; but even in music the range of composers during the past fifty years has not been as great as that of the eighteenth century, because until to-day new composers could not forget the old.

The Press, which sometimes claims to speak the public mind or to lead it, is generally reduced to platitudes or irrelevancies when public policy is the subject. Perhaps indeed a newspaper is nothing but an advertisement sheet for which the largest sale is desirable; but if it is a part of the Spiritual Power, then it fails to distinguish the trivial from the fundamental, or to give any perspective to the mind of the common man. The theatres, cinemas, music halls, dance halls, and other places of entertainment have supplied some relief from the routine of industrial life; but they have hardly begun to criticize or satirize contemporary bad habits or to express nobilities of character.

Clearly such an attack upon the institutions of the Spiritual Power in contemporary life implies that these institutions have a greater function to perform than making evils endurable. But it is also implied that there is no compulsion or pressure on the part of the common man to prevent the exceptional men in these institutions from producing a finer art or a nobler type of character. For if it is said that democracy would not supply a livelihood to a great artist, then it is assumed that the great artist must be very unskilful in inducing anyone else to see that he is great.

The failure of the Spiritual Power may be expressed in two ways. It may be said to have adopted for its gospel the cries of the market-place and to have sought success or support from those whom it should have criticized. Or it may be said to have made the "great refusal", which Dante cursed, in avoiding all issues which are vital. Both charges are true. The Churches and the Universities in many countries have made themselves the instruments of the crudest nationalism and the most insolent autocracy. The learned and literary world has made itself into a footstool for vulgar riches.[1] But the other charge is more deadly. The flunkeyism of some leaders of organized religion and accepted culture is of small importance by comparison to the guilty silence of most of them when common men needed guidance. The chief complaint therefore made against the Spiritual Power to-day is that it has not used the opportunities which its position in society conferred upon it.

Men of exceptional insight or creative ability are parts of a community whose blood courses through their veins. And the failure to recognize the social soil in which their abilities grow is a defect in insight. To require the "guardians" of a community not to depart into the clouds and, according to the Platonic doctrine, to expect service from them, is not unjust; for originality owes much to commonplace. Even a genius needs boots and bread, and does not disdain to receive them from common men. It is childish for the superior person to condemn the dustman for his lack of culture, so long as this superior person does not remove his own refuse. But the complacency of the over-educated is incurable.

There may be many explanations of the failure of the Spiritual Power, but probably the best is—traditionalism. True, there may be in any generation no adequate supply of artistic or

[1] See Jacques Benda, *La Trahison des clercs*. But I by no means accept his conclusion that the "clerc" should be removed out of the battle.

scientific genius: or, again, such ability as exists in a changing society may be exhausted in politics and industry, leaving nothing for religion, art, or science. For some defects of character and conduct in any society no one is to be blamed. Natural circumstances may not permit the birth of genius. But some failures of ability are due to mistakes of actual men and women, who had the possibilities of success. For example, the development of character and conduct through education may be traditionalist, or it may be revolutionary. That is to say, the schools may model the new generation on the old, or they may boldly attempt a new form. But during the recent past education has been so much concerned with "handing on a tradition" of knowledge and conduct that it has not fitted men to face new issues. In that sense the failure of the Spiritual Power is due to the mistaken judgments of actual men and women. They have thought of civilized life only in terms of what has already been achieved.

But if another type of civilized life is possible under the influence of the democratic ideal, then the use of the arts and sciences and religion must depend upon the experience of the common man. The structure of society must be such as to include a place for the functioning of the Spiritual Power. Politics and industry must not exhaust all the available abilities; and, just as in those sections of social life so also in culture, the common man must provide more than a following.

The arts and sciences and religion, in its widest sense, are necessary in a democratic society because, first, they extend the actual perceptiveness of common men, and because, secondly, they give him a sense of his unused powers. In the first place, then, democracy involves the bringing into play of abilities to see and hear, act and speak, which the common man does not yet contribute; and painting and music, for example, are means for the opening of eyes and ears. Therefore they are necessary means for attaining democracy. But the argument must not be misinterpreted. Art is not only or mainly an instrument of illumination. Its "educational" value is incidental, as in the case of a sunset, whose beauty does not exist for the sake of the emotion it may excite. The true artist is very seldom consciously a teacher. The work of art is normally the result of an inner impulse, seeking a form in material, which form, when found, does indeed communicate the impulse to others; but the communication is of minor importance in explaining the work of art itself. Nevertheless, for the purpose of the argument here, which is concerned with the common man, it is most important that he is affected by art so as to see and feel more keenly. Any man who has been "moved" by a Constable drawing of a cloud will see clouds better and other things also. Any man who has been "moved" by a Beethoven melody will be able to hear melodies underlying the noises of industrial life. But if common men become more sensitive, they will be unable to endure the ancient evils, poverty and war. The survival of the traditions maintaining these evils is due partly to insensitiveness, which accepts as inevitable what is not deeply disturbing. And short of the destruction of great evils, a more delicate susceptibility to beauty would compel men to abolish ugliness and noise. Thus, even indirectly, the arts would civilize a democratic society, if the organized Spiritual Power fulfilled its true function.

A second incidental effect of the arts, sciences, and religion is the strengthening or vitalizing of the common man; and here again obviously democracy is concerned, since contributions to the common life are much greater if they come from persons alive at all points. This vitalizing seems to be derived from a sense that, if one can see so well as being affected by art indicates, then one has forces within still unused. A certain self-confidence is derived from the expansiveness of personality under the influence of the Spiritual Power; for it is a perversion of Christianity and of any true religion to make it into a doctrine of resignation. All true religion is revolutionary, in so far as it makes men feel that the world is not worthy of them.

The conception of Heaven or of Nirvana, mythological as all such expressions may be, is nevertheless a reminder to the "true believer" that his home is not in the circumstances of the moment. This implies a citizenship in a City of God, whose ambassadors the officials or representatives of the Spiritual Power are supposed to be. But the sense among common men that they have another citizenship, besides that in daily circumstance, gives them power to transform these circumstances and themselves. The power derived from insight into factors that are not superficial, is not to be rendered only or mainly in terms of social reform.[1] A certain quality of character and conduct, which was once called gentility and perhaps in some obscure sense saintliness, is the finest product of the ability to perceive what is not obvious. The change in the quality of reformers is more important for civilized life than the excellence of their schemes for reform; for no great deeds can be done by small men. But democracy needs a larger company of great men than any other form of society, and their greatness in a democracy is not a capacity for catching the limelight.

But the most important aspect of the influence of the Spiritual Power in a democracy is the possible proof, which its influence might secure, that a democracy can produce a civilized life at least as fine as any hitherto developed. Such a proof could only be given if the works of art so produced were as fine as any in the past; for the quality of a civilization is at least partly indicated by its arts. But since no democratic community has yet existed, obviously no actual examples of a democratic art or religion can be cited. The proof that such art or religion, if they did occur, would be finer than those under an oligarchic system lies in the analysis of the source of inspiration in great works of genius; for it seems probable that art

[1] H. G. Wells, in *The Open Conspiracy*, limits the meaning of religion too much. Religion affects not merely social structure or custom, but the *quality* of personality.

and religion which grows in the common soil has a more vigorous life than such art and religion as is the product of a small group of superior persons. The deeper the roots, the higher the branches of the tree. Art which is *déraciné* is trivial. Folk melody is the source of divine harmonies. And even in the case of science—the science which is not continually revived by contact with commonplace utility, like a giant in the old legend falling on the earth, soon becomes an empty formula. That is at least one of the reasons why the abolition of Latin as a learned language accompanied a revival of science.[1] It follows that the artist and scientist and religious genius should not cut themselves off from the common man—not merely because of their duties to him but also because art, science, and religion are likely to rise to greater heights when the sap of common experience runs through them. But this implies a confidence in the common man which is still rare among those who have exceptional insight or ability; and the common man himself may have to compel that confidence. It is already so compelled in the minds of all those who can perceive the fine quality of sympathy and the endurance of pain and death and the delight in beauty among Nobodies!

[1] Condorcet's *Sketch of Human History* contains the most eloquent statement of this argument.

CHAPTER XI

THE DEMOCRATIC MAN

WHATEVER the defects of a democratic society, it has this great advantage, that it can be criticized freely. Criticism is not allowed in oligarchies, nor in modern tyrannies such as Fascism or Russian Communism. Democracy shows its inner strength by allowing adverse criticism. But to criticize democracy because it has not yet produced the finest civilization implies a belief that in common men is a greater force than has been yet used. Such criticism is intended to release those powers for good which are concealed by habits and traditional institutions; for the fundamental issue is not what kind of institutions are best, but what kind of men and women.

It is quite useless to give everyone "a say", if no one has anything of value to say; and a system which requires the daily support of common men is futile, if most of them are weak-willed or unwilling. Undoubtedly in communities claiming to be democratic to-day men wait to be spoon-fed and then grumble at the food. The voice of "the people" is often only an echo of some Stentor of the Press; and this is not always due to the operation of mass influence or mob mind. It is sometimes due to inert intelligence or sodden emotions in Smith and Jones and their wives. The success or failure of the democratic ideal depends, therefore, not only on the institutions which give the opportunities for the abilities of the common man to come into play, but also upon the actual release of more force—more varied and more effectual co-operation by individuals. Clearly as institutions become more elaborate, the chances of error in social action become more numerous; but on the other hand, each error is less disastrous in proportion as the whole of social life is made up of contributions from many men. In the life of a community the katabolism, the wearing down due to the inertia or unintelligence of some, is repaired by the anabolism of energy and interest shown by others. The balance of the two tendencies, towards decay and towards growth, is difficult to adjust in any society; but in a democracy it depends upon thousands of common men and women, and in order that a democratic society should grow and not decay these men and women must be interested enough in its future to add to its store of vitality whatever little abilities they may possess. In an oligarchy or tyranny the vitality of the whole group may come from a few: the inertia of the many may be a positive advantage. But in a democracy the common man must be lively in perception and alert in action.

A particular kind of man and woman, therefore, is needed in a democratic society, by contrast with the types which are useful in other social conditions. In an oligarchy or dictatorship, for example, the types of men needed are, first, great numbers of reverential, obedient, and uncritical instruments, and secondly, a few self-confident givers of orders.[1] Such a society may run trains very well and even work hard at producing goods; but it cuts down the possible supply of intelligence, insight, and emotion, available for the common life, and it puts a very great strain upon those who have to give orders to fellow-men who are unable to criticize such orders and are therefore reduced to the level of dumb beasts. The "levelling down" of the majority in an oligarchy or a dictatorship is inevitable, for to treat men as animals or as tools makes them so. And, on the other hand, the very self-confidence of a dictator narrows his outlook. There are abundant examples in history and in contemporary life of the excellences and defects of a subject population under a benevolent tyranny; and the argument against tyranny is strongest if the tyranny is assumed to be benevolent. The squire and the parson,

[1] The use of the word "reverential" in what follows here will remind students of political philosophy of Bagehot's theory of the "reverential" elements in Great Britain, which in more brutal terms may be called "flunkeyism". Bagehot's argument is implied to be wrong.

who guide the peasant feel, no doubt, responsibility for the peasant's good; but if the function of the peasant is reduced to listening to lessons, the squire and the parson lack the evidence for discovering what is the peasant's good. Again, the peasantry which transfers reverentially to others the responsibility for considering the common good is diminished in its manhood, and is therefore a less valuable instrument of that good. Other types of social life, then, require other types of men: what type is required for democracy?

In a democratic, as in every other society, the normal psychological types will be found. At least there will be (1) the good-tempered, easily influenced, custom-following man, and (2) the ill-adjusted, critical, or original man, who in the extreme state is, as the psychologists say, "schizophrenic".[1] Between these two extreme types the majority of common men will fall into many psychological classes, which will differ in their numbers in different countries, climates, or economic and political circumstances. But it is not possible here to attempt a descriptive psychological classification of any community, which is clearly required before any generalizations are made about "national character" or differences between the French, the British, and the Americans. It is enough if every society be assumed to include both the easy-going and the critical. In a democratic society the daily round will depend upon the former. They are sociable, clubbable, tending to associate and to work together. They enjoy working together. Indeed, a "common purpose", as it is called, is often simply an excuse for indulging the desire to work with others; and in such cases it is not the purpose which gives a meaning to the association, but the association which excuses the purpose.[2] For example, men do not like war; but they like fellowship

[1] See Emmanuel Miller, *Types of Mind and Body*, and Jung, *Psychological Types*, etc.

[2] It is doubtful whether this psychological factor is allowed for in Hetherington and Muirhead's *Social Purpose*.

in armies. Men do not normally aim at the good life through social co-operation; they enjoy good fellowship and call its incidental consequences the good life. It is not denied that many men do work for wealth or power, nor that all men desire to be happy. The point is that for most common men happiness is generally found in the experience of fellowship. On the other hand, (2) the schizophrenic may not be actually "unhinged", but they are less reliable than their fellows. The reference is not now only to genius or to exceptional ability, which indeed is often associated with instability of temperament; for the common man also may be schizophrenic. There are some who would not be happy in heaven—even a heaven devised by themselves. They are not sociable, for they think best and feel most keenly alone. They require a certain "insulation" from their fellow-men. Among men of that kind are usually to be found the opponents of democracy in democratic countries. But in other countries they advocate democracy. It would be disastrous if a democratic society could not find a place for such men and women, for they make revolutions, and they are also the best artists and scientists. They initiate the "breakaway" which develops new customs out of old habits. They are the growth-point of a community. Their song is:

> O nations undivided! O single peoples and free!
> We dreamers, we derided, we mad blind men that see,
> We bear you witness ere you come,
> That you shall be.

Thus among men who seem to have no special competence or ability there are some who are easily influenced by a new idea, who readily adopt unconventional habits; and a democratic society more than any other would have a place for such men. In any case, there is no possibility of destroying that type in any form of society.

But besides the kinds of men that every society must include, there are some kinds which distinguish democracy from other forms of society. The psychological types "cocksure" and reverential are not suitable for the co-operation of equals; but in a democratic society there should be at least two characteristics in the outlook and conduct of all men; first, a sturdy independence, and, secondly, imaginative sympathy. By independence is meant not a blustering individualism, but the desire to avoid being a burden to anyone. Individualism is entirely opposed to such independence; for it claims recognition for one's self. It asserts its right to use service. It assumes that others are its instruments or that it deserves well. The independent man, on the other hand, is shy, silent, grateful for services he does not claim but needs. An independent man will avoid being in the way of others and will do the best he can without calling for help: he is valiant but not defiant; self-confident but not assertive; and there are millions of such men and women in poor houses, in workshops, and in streets. Naturally, they are not noticed by journalists or demagogues or superior persons who look only for what catches the limelight. They are, however, well enough known to their friends; and their gospel, too bitterly phrased indeed, but not acid, is in the sonnet of the blind poet, Philip Marsden:

> Of me ye may say many a bitter thing,
> O men, when I am gone, gone far away
> To that dim land where shines no light of day.
> Sharp was the bread for my soul's nourishing
> Which Fate allowed; and bitter was the spring
> Of which I drank and maddened, even as they
> Who, wild with thirst at sea, will not delay
> But drink the brine and die of its sharp sting.
>
> Not gentle was my war with Chance; and yet
> I borrowed no man's sword. Alone I drew
> And gave my dead fit burial out of view.
> In secret places I and sorrow met;
> So when you count my sins, do not forget
> To say I taxed not any one of you.

A democratic society will need men and women who have this characteristic independence; for it implies that the life of each common man is in his own eyes and hands. Authoritarianism rests upon subservience to guidance on the part of those who feel their incompetence. The common man in a democratic society does not claim to know metaphysics or to be expert in details of public policy, but he values more highly the vigour of his own feet than the external direction he may need for their best use. He may often go wrong because he goes with inadequate guidance, but he goes. And the subservient waits to be pushed. Independence, then, in the sense in which the word is here used, implies vitality.

Clearly existing societies claiming to be democratic do not include many who have vitality of this kind. Even the young are generally inert, without interest or energy for anything but momentary excitement. But it is implied in the argument that this deficiency is due to early education and to material circumstances. With a greater skill in education, therefore, men could become more independent.

The independent man is the ideal of character and conduct implied in the advocacy of liberty, and of equality as its basis. In the United States and in the British Dominions that type of man and woman occurs more frequently and counts for more than in older societies. The type is commoner in the north of England and in Scotland than in the south of England or in Germany. Certain kinds of education, occupation, and social custom tend to produce the independent man; and in that far they are democratic. But it would be a mistake to accept independence as the only characteristic of the democratic man, for two reasons: first, because most men who are thus independent, without having the second quality to which reference is made below, are unconscious of the amount of common prejudice, belief, or custom on which their independence rests, and, secondly, because independence uncorrected by social perceptiveness dissolves or weakens social bonds. Hence the apparently contradictory phenomena in America and other new countries, where men who claim and praise independence are very intolerant of any criticism of what they themselves do not feel to be a bondage. Independent thought is often abhorrent to men who claim complete freedom, in their sense of the word, for themselves. Hence also countries of independent men are often countries without competent or honest government, for government appears to be a side-issue, if everyone is satisfied that he can do everything for himself.

America has embodied the liberty of the democratic ideal and almost forgotten the fraternity which was once supposed to be its complement. Worse still, independence turning into individualism has covered its tracks with clouds of "uplift", lofty platitudes about a "fraternity" which is neither privately practised nor embodied in institutions. Thus in new countries only one half of the democratic ideal has been achieved; and as in private relations society seems to be only a collection of independent atoms, so the relation of States is conceived in new countries to be best when each State goes its own way. The democratic ideal is therefore misrepresented because only one element in it is understood: autonomy is taken to mean independence without obligations. But it cannot be too strongly stated that a democratic man or a democratic community is not only one which is independent but also one which is imaginatively sympathetic.

Secondly, therefore, a democratic society needs men and women with imaginative sympathy. This is the complement, in terms of character and conduct, of independence; for having such sympathy a man who asks for nothing is ready to give what he can. Imaginative sympathy, again, is common in trains and shops and streets among quite ordinary folk; but its value for democracy in politics and industry is hardly recognized and clearly it must be more highly developed if the democratic ideal is to be effectual. It involves an understanding by each that, for example, in politics he cannot refuse to help, on the ground that his help is small. In industry, a man with imaginative sympathy feels that the other working at his elbow is at the same game in the same team, and that the boot he is making will be worn by somebody. True, the complexity of modern government and industry requires the "reach" of imaginative sympathy to be much more extensive and much more subtle than it was in village life. But the present skill in such sympathy, that is in acts, not in vague sentimentalism—may be increased. Education for a democracy is not to give people "airs", but to give them tolerance. It should at least give them an interest in their fellow-men. No man has any right to be dull; and the only way of being "interesting" is to be "interested".

Imaginative sympathy has actually increased in the past century. The barbaric public executions of the eighteenth century have been abolished and men shrink from war as they never did before. This is humanitarian benevolence, in so far as it involves pity for the sufferings of others; and it is extended in democratic societies even to animals. But it is more than benevolence when it forestalls possible pain which might be caused by one's own act. Imaginative sympathy, then, embodies a sense of justice or of the rights of others. Such sympathy does not "condescend" towards the sufferer. It is an attitude of reverence for such courage as appears in the bearing of pain, such endurance as most industrial services entail. But imaginative sympathy does not depend upon the existence of evil, as humanitarianism may; for a man may sympathize with the enjoyment of others. In a democratic society this would prevail over the desire to model others on one's self. Imaginative sympathy may be an appreciation of what the other man is going to do before he does it; and for that reason the man who has sympathy is the best for the co-operation which is democratic.

Thus no society can be fairly called democratic, in the full sense of that word, which is defective in social perceptiveness expressed in actions. America and other new countries are too individualistic to be democratic, although greater skill in that form of co-operation which is called government is developing quickly there. Long ago it was remarked that the tendency to associate in groups for common purposes is a characteristic of democracy:[1] but clubs do not make a community, nor charitable institutions a government. In Great Britain and perhaps also in France the sense of the community, both civic and national, is very strong; and it acts as a corrective of political corruption or extreme "party politics". But this sense of the community, operating in institutions or daily acts of the common man, is the imaginative sympathy which is one aspect of democracy. Its weakness is that men in that tradition look to public institutions as props or saviours or "providences": if evil comes, they blame "the government", not their own inertia; if they desire good, they expect "the government" to provide it. What is wrong, with private enterprise, for example, in Great Britain is mainly that, however private it is, it is not enterprise. But the co-operation essential in a democratic community cannot be merely the habit that each man has, of leaning up against the others. Independence may turn into an unjustifiable isolation: but imaginative sympathy may become only waiting for someone else to act. Co-operation involves initiative in each member of the community.

In the relation of groups, whether industrial or national, imaginative sympathy would involve that each group plays into the other's hands. Thus the policy of peace would be, not the creation of some new super-State, to take over from Great Britain, France, Germany, and the rest, the organization of the world, but the interlocking of the administrative machinery of the several existing States under the guidance of a policy with a common objective and many instruments. But this, again, requires that the common man in each nation should conceive his own Government as an instrument for the good of the citizens of other Governments, and should

[1] See de Tocqueville, *Democracy in America.*

look to other Governments as likely to be of advantage to him.

It follows that not merely by education, but by continuous practice every day, the art of living in a democracy must be perfected. The essential need is for an increase of social skill, which depends upon perceptiveness in regard to personality. But there is no better means of attaining such perceptiveness than what used to be called "the humanities". In education in schools or universities, literature and history are essential for a democracy. Clearly the sciences are valuable for other purposes; because men need to know the conditions under which they must devise their control of their own lives and the forces available for such a purpose. But the purpose itself is not learnt from the sciences; and the methods by which men, as contrasted with nature, are best understood are not mathematical nor descriptive. The utility of the physical and the social sciences is generally admitted. It is useful to have better instruments for civilized life and still more useful to have minds trained as only exact science can train them. But the qualities and characteristics of human beings are to be discovered most easily in the humanities; and this use of the humanities does not cease after the school and the university have done their best.

The humanities, in this sense, do not give information about facts but appreciation of values. The best result of reading Plato, for example, is not the knowledge of his doctrine, but the acquaintance with such a man. So it is in all great literature. To become aware of men whose "converse" is such philosophy or poetry is to acquire an appreciation of what men can be; and to enter into such a company is to belong to the City of God. A man who is accustomed to such company has an indefinable air, which is not that of the superior person, but of one susceptible to finer issues and percipient of the less obvious factors in human experience.

It is only too obvious that education in history and literature became in the eighteenth century, if not before, a mere acquisition of superficial graces. The gentleman in the Palace of Versailles had little indeed of that more democratic *vera gentilezza* of which Dante wrote. But the education connected with the study of dead languages and the security from popular criticism which platitudes in an unknown tongue may attain, are not the results of a genuine study of the humanities. The deepest and most enduring effects of a great personality, through his art, are to be found in the attitude towards other men, which those who understand his work may develop.

Again, the democratic man will be formed by the humanities because they are the means of breaking down those barriers which maintain provincialism and village politics. Literature and the other arts cannot possibly be supposed to exist only in one's own country, or only in one's own age. Now the growth of small groups is obvious in modern life; but if such groups "harden", one against the other, democracy is impossible, because too many obstacles to co-operation arise. The humanities are useful in overcoming the differences between groups, formed by diverse occupations or dwelling-places.

Acquaintance with literature and appreciation of works of fine art, then, are not only useful, they are essential to democracy; for they are the means by which that skill in social intercourse is acquired which is the life-blood of a democratic community. By such means the independence described above may be secured, because one gains an understanding of depths and strengths in one's own personality under the influence of the arts. Contact with greatness brings out what is great in what is common. And secondly, by such means one acquires a more subtle and more intensive imaginative sympathy, because art makes intelligible in other persons what is otherwise opaque. "A 'real' person, profoundly as we may sympathize with him, is in a great measure perceptible only through our senses; that is to say, he remains opaque, offers a dead weight which our sensibilities have not the strength to lift. . . . The novelist's happy discovery was to substitute for these opaque sections, impenetrable to the human spirit, their equivalent in immaterial sections, things, that is, which the spirit can assimilate to itself."[1]

The democratic man, then, or the man characteristic of a democratic society will be both independent and sympathetic. There will be, of course, in such a society a great variety of ability or competence; but the qualities so far discussed are conceived not as special virtues of a few, but as belonging to the common man. This is not creation out of nothing. The material in common folk is already abundant and ductible. The poets have seen it and it has been described thus:

> The well-born, the clever, the haughty, the greedy in their fear, pride and wilfulness, and the perplexity of their scheming, make a mess of the world. Forthwith in their panic they cry: "Calamity cometh!" Then out of their obscurity, where they dwelt because of their low worth, arise the Nobodies: because theirs is the historic job of restoring again the upset balance of affairs. They make no fuss about it. Theirs is always the hard and dirty work. They have always done it. If they don't do it, it will not be done. They fall with a will and without complaint upon the wreckage made of generations of such labour as theirs, to get the world right again, to make it habitable again—not for themselves.
>
> About you and me there are men like that. There is nothing to distinguish them. They show no sign of greatness. They have common talk. They walk with an ugly lurch. Their eyes are not eager. They are not polite. Their clothes are dirty. They live in cheap houses on cheap food. They are the great unwashed, the inevitable many, the common people. Greatness is as common as that.[2]
>
> The knowledge that there are such men gives to an aimless and sprawling world the assurance of anonymous courage and faith waiting in the sordid muddle for a signal, ready when it comes. There are men like that. You can never tell where they are. They are only the crowd. There is nothing to distinguish them. They have no names. They are nobodies. But when they are wanted, there they are; and when they have finished their task, they disappear, leaving no sign except in the heart. Without the certainty of that artless and profitless

[1] See Proust, *Swan's Way*, vol. i, p. 113, Eng. Trans.

[2] H. M. Tomlinson, *Old Junk*, pp. 200 and 77.

> fidelity of simple souls the great ocean would be as silly as the welter of doom undesigned and the shining importance of the august affairs of the flourishing cities worth no more homage than the brickbats of Babylon. These people give to God the only countenance by which he can be known.[1]

Here, then, is the beginning of that democratic society envisaged in the argument of this book. It would be foolish indeed to calculate only in terms of institutions the chances of making the democratic ideal more effectual. The abolition of poverty, the obsolescence of war, and the release of those unused abilities on which democracy must rely—all depend ultimately upon the existence of a certain heroism among common men, which is the reasonable ground for the beliefs that the present social system can be drastically altered. Secondly, the democratic man is shown to be a possibility by the experience of the past fifty years in those countries in which the democratic ideal has been operative. The defects of such communities have been admitted; and yet not only in mechanisms and institutions but also in manners and customs, the contrast is startling between the "tone" of life to-day and what it was even fifty years ago. And if that contrast is not admitted to be in favour of social life to-day, at least it should be admitted that with the transformation of custom, industrialized communities have entered into an unexplored country. Thus, if Athens and Florence and eighteenth-century Paris could not produce fine arts and the graces of culture without subservience and autocracy, that is no proof that it can never be done. The whole situation is altered. How deeply it is altered no one can understand who lives among the books of the dead. On the other hand, a negative is a lame conclusion. The dependence of Athens on oligarchy does not prove that oligarchy is essential in all circumstances to civilization; but this means only that a democratic civilization may exist, not that it will. That a democratic civilization will arise is

[1] H. M. Tomlinson, *Gallions Reach*, p. 170.

shown to be probable because the immense change recently made has been made under the domination of the democratic ideal; and that change, although it has not yet produced music and painting greater than the old, has already secured greater vitality from which greater achievements may reasonably be expected. Those who worked for the transformation of the past fifty years were not titled, nor privileged; and they have worked in groups, not in Napoleonic aloofness. The epic of the common man has yet to be written; but the results of his work are around us. There is no conclusive proof that the future will be better than the past, and recent success is not evidence that it will continue: every step, however, has released new vitality, and the abilities of the common man are by no means exhausted.

Rivers of energy and good fellowship in common men are still held frozen by an ice-age of suspicion and jealousy. Fear, like a frost, keeps nation armed against nation—fear, which lives upon the ignorance of common men as to other common men's joys and sorrows. Fear to lose a little keeps men from the only acts which will abolish poverty—that is not giving, but hesitating to take. Men hold tightly the little good they have, each for himself—blind to the common good in which all could share. But the ice-age is passing; for not only by new laws or new institutions, but also by the acts of Nobodies the democratic ideal becomes daily more operative and the minds of men are freed from fear. In the hands of the Nobodies is the hope of the future.

BIBLIOGRAPHY

(*a*) Criticism.

Lord Bryce: *Modern Democracies*. 2 vols. 1921. (Macmillan.)

H. J. Laski: *Grammar of Politics*. (Allen & Unwin.)

Clive Bell: *Civilization*. (Chatto & Windus.)

R. M. McIver: *Community*. (Macmillan.)

T. P. Nunn: *Education*. (Arnold.)

H. G. Wells: *The Open Conspiracy*. (Gollancz.)

Emile Faguet: *The Cult of Incompetence* (trans.).

R. H. Tawney: *The Acquisitive Society*. (Bell.)

John Dewey: *The Public and its Problems*. 1927. (Allen & Unwin.)

J. A. Hobson: *Wealth and Life*. 1929. (Macmillan.)

(*b*) Speculation.

C. Kapek: *R. U. R. and the Insect Play* (trans. Oxford Press).

Paul Valery: *Eupalinos*.

G. B. Shaw: *Back to Methuselah*.

Willa Cather: *Death comes to the Archbishop*.

Frank Thiess: *Das Gesicht des Jahrhunderts*.

INDEX